Hamlet

.

HAMLET

A Guide to the Play

W. THOMAS MACCARY

Greenwood Guides to Shakespeare

Greenwood Press
Westport, Connecticut • London

Library of Congress Cataloging-in-Publication Data

MacCary, W. Thomas.
    Hamlet : a guide to the play / W. Thomas MacCary.
      p. cm. — (Greenwood guides to Shakespeare)
    Includes bibliographical references and index.
    ISBN 0–313–30082–8 (alk. paper)
    1. Shakespeare, William, 1564–1616.—Hamlet—Handbooks, manuals,
etc. 2. Denmark—In literature—Handbooks, manuals, etc.
3. Princes in literature—Handbooks, manuals, etc. 4. Tragedy—
Handbooks, manuals, etc. I. Title. II. Series.
PR2807.M28   1998
822.3′3—dc21   97–38987

British Library Cataloguing in Publication Data is available.

Library of Congress Catalog Card Number: 97–38987
ISBN: 0–313–30082–8

First published in 1998

Greenwood Press, 88 Post Road West, Westport, CT 06881
An imprint of Greenwood Publishing Group, Inc.

Printed in the United States of America

The paper used in this book complies with the
Permanent Paper Standard issued by the National
Information Standards Organization (Z39.48–1984).

10 9 8 7 6 5 4 3 2 1

*In memory of
Ann Weissberg,
my Horatio.*

CONTENTS

PREFACE

This series provides Shakespeare readers and playgoers with scholarly and critical information that will enhance their experience of the individual plays. Most modern editions of the plays contain some kind of critical introduction and footnotes of an explanatory nature. In this book more comprehensive information is laid out in a format that allows readers to refer immediately to the item of interest, for example, "Historical Context," "Television Performances," and so on. In this way, the book serves as a true reference work. At the same time, because *Hamlet* is the most complex and controversial of all works of literature, what is said in one section is often supplemented and expanded in another, so there is need of *cross*-reference. The chapters in this book are essentially discrete essays that build on each other, beginning with consideration of the earliest editions of *Hamlet* and ending with the most recent productions. (All of the quotations from *Hamlet* are taken from *The Arden Shakespeare*, edited by H. Jenkins, unless otherwise noted.) There are two main organizing principles: *Hamlet* exists in history and so changes; *Hamlet* is both text and performance, or, under the most favorable circumstances, a function of the interaction of the two. The subtleties of the text are realized in performance by actors and directors who constantly question and test the play's infinite potential for meaning.

INTRODUCTION

Hamlet is always with us. Even those who have never read the complete play or seen a performance know a few lines of "To be or not to be" and recognize the image of a young man contemplating the skull of his dead friend Yorick. *Hamlet* thus exists in three dimensions: as text, performance, and cultural icon. In the chapters that follow, these three different *Hamlet*s will be distinguished but also considered together. If the elements of this play have become clichés, that is because the play as a whole continues to fascinate us all, defining some essential aspect of our own experience. The relation between the play itself and the popular conception of its hero is like the relation between tragedy and myth in the ancient Greek experience: the Greek audience would enter the theatre to see Sophocles' *Oedipus Tyrannos* for the first time already knowing the myth, or plot, of the play. We do the same too. Freud has made the experience of Oedipus so familiar to us that we know him before we see his play. And, of course, during the hundred years of the psychoanalytic movement, Hamlet has been compared with Oedipus: the young man seeks vengeance for his father's murder but somehow feels conflicted, as if he himself were complicitous in that murder rather than purely and simply his father's avenger.

Recently Disney produced *The Lion King*, an animated feature that traces the adventures of a lion cub's coming to maturity and taking his place at the head of his pride, as his father had done before him. The authors of this screenplay knew *Hamlet* well. They provide an evil uncle, who convinces the young hero that he is responsible for his father's death; this sends him into a deep depression, and he wastes away his adolescence with companions who have no purpose in life other than pleasure. Finally, under the influence of a wise, old prophet, the hero returns to the pride, takes vengeance on his uncle—who has been revealed as his father's actual murderer and is now ruling in his place—and assumes his rightful role as Lion King. One would not have thought that *Hamlet* was appropriate fare for children, and yet, in this treatment of the basic outline of the story, we see its dimension as a parable for youth. Every young person has ambivalent feelings about his or her parents—respect and admiration compounded with impatience and resentment: when will he or she be independent of them, indeed, take their place? All of this is intensified if—as is almost always the case in fairy tales, and, as Aristotle observes, in tragedy—the parents are king and queen and the child is prince or princess. Royal succession then becomes an exaggerated statement for coming of age.

The differences between Shakespeare's *Hamlet* and the Disney adaptation are just as interesting as the similarities. Most important is the ending. Whereas Shakespeare's hero, though finally driven to effect his vengeance on his uncle, dies in the process, the Lion King rules happily ever after. Thus the adaptation carries two important moral lessons for youth: stand up for what is right (the killing of the uncle is left to the vicious hyenas) and accept responsibility as part of maturity. Notoriously, Hamlet is not the eighteen-year-old we would expect to come home from college for his father's funeral; the chronology given in the gravediggers' scene (Act V, scene i) proves him to be over thirty. Through four long acts, he delays and delays in seeking vengeance, and finally seems forced into it by circumstance. When he actually kills his uncle, it is not in vengeance for his uncle's having killed his father, but rather for his uncle's having plotted to kill Hamlet himself. We must appreciate that tragedy insists on consistency of character. Whereas in lesser genres a happy ending can be tacked on to seemingly serious concerns, in tragedy the hero determines the outcome of the action. In Shakespeare's source for *Hamlet*, the hero did assume the rule, and only after a long reign did he fall victim to a plot against his life. Shakespeare foreshortened this in order to emphasize not that tragedy must end in death but that the tragic hero cannot drastically change in character. His death must be "deserved"; we must come to appreciate that it is somehow inevitable that he and his uncle die together. Again, if we compare Hamlet with Oedipus, we see the inevitability of Oedipus's blinding himself: he had cursed the man who killed his father, and he finally realizes that he is that man. We must also consider the proposition that *Hamlet* is not pure tragedy; the hero becomes a victim of circumstances beyond his control and thus presents an image to us of our own helplessness under the forces of history rather than of the power of the individual to shape his or her destiny, no matter how such pressure operates on the hero.

Something essential to *Hamlet* that was left out of the Disney adaptation is the hero's ambivalence toward his mother. From the first soliloquy, we realize that Hamlet is more distraught by his mother's marriage to his uncle than by his father's death. He feels betrayed, and his sense of disgust with her clouds his vision of the world at large. Thus Shakespeare presents us with the play's greatest paradox: somehow the hero's inability to avenge his father's murder is tied up with his hatred of his mother. It is almost as if nothing is worth doing in the world now that he knows his mother is unfaithful. He seems to associate his mother with the world as it is—shallow and corrupt—and his father with the world as it should be. His mother is all flesh, representing change and decay, and his father is now spirit, representing constant perfection. We see this division extended to other characters. Hamlet dismisses the innocent young Ophelia as a whore, assimilating her to his mother, and he idolizes Horatio as the perfectly honest man, unchanging in the contrary winds of fortune.

The complexity of Hamlet's character then arranges itself around two poles: misogyny and idealism. He hates women because he associates them with change and deception: they paint their faces, they say one thing and mean another, and they pretend to love their husbands but then seek sexual satisfaction wherever they can find it. In fact, they are sexually insatiable—so driven by desire that they will say or do anything. This drives Hamlet to thoughts of death as an escape from such a world of appetite and hypocrisy. But then he thinks of the Christian hell, where souls are damned for murder and suicide to eternal torment. His inability to act is then doubly determined: nothing in this life is worth doing, and certainly nothing is worth doing that costs the soul damnation in the next life. Another way he looks at his dilemma is as two different types of torment: here and now he is buffeted about by faithless friends and willful women; hereafter he fears the turmoil of the underworld as described in Christian mythology and by his father's ghost when it comes to demand revenge. What Hamlet really wants is calm and certainty; perhaps we should associate these features with his life of study at Wittenberg. He feels he has been thrust into the world of court intrigue unprepared. His nature tends toward the quiet contemplation of eternal truths rather than the hugger-mugger of daily life.

The polarities are then youthful repose—a university education used to mean withdrawal from the world to a cloistered existence for the study of philosophy and theology—and mature engagement; ageless and changeless values as opposed to the compromises required in active life; the embrace of a childhood friend of the same sex rather than risking the uncertainties of commitment to a member of the opposite sex. These are the tensions that Hamlet feels, familiar to us all but heightened in his case because of his peculiar circumstances: he is a prince, and his mother, the Queen, has married his father's murderer, who has now become the King. Claudius tries to explain his overhasty marriage to Gertrude as an expedient to unify Denmark against the threat of invasion by Norway. In Shakespeare's source, Hamlet's mother is descended from the royal line. In the Oedipus myth, the hero kills the old king on his way to Thebes, solves the riddle of the Sphinx when he arrives, and then marries the old king's wife. The woman has the power to throw a cloak of legitimacy over usurpation, almost as if there were a hint of matrilineal succession. Considering that *Hamlet* was first produced in the last years of Elizabeth I's reign, when she refused to name a successor, we might decide that Shakespeare exploits the myth of women's political power. Indeed he identifies sexual power and political power: the man who is strong enough to satisfy the woman has the right to rule in the land. Hamlet is ambivalent about both sex and politics, again showing the reluctance of the very young man to enter into the affairs of his father.

Through close attention to the language, structure, and background of the play, and an attempt to visualize its action on stage, we should be able to appreciate how Shakespeare related these different themes and conventions. Perhaps we shall find that he suggests a resolution: Hamlet, even though his character does not drastically change, reaches an understanding of his situation which gives him finally some control over his destiny.

1

TEXTUAL HISTORY

Hamlet as text is a problem in evolution. Two editions were printed in Shakespeare's lifetime (First and Second Quartos) and another in a memorial volume of his complete works prepared by friends and colleagues just seven years after his death (First Folio). These three early editions present modern editors with great challenges to both theory and practice: how are they related, and which should be followed in the reading of a particular passage? In a simplified overview of the intricacies of this tradition, we can see that it began with and has now returned to the principle of discrimination, whereas during the late seventeenth through the early twentieth centuries there was a tendency toward conflation—an amalgamated *Hamlet*, as it were. Now editors discriminate among the early editions, the two most influential (both Oxford and Cambridge) preferring the First Folio on the grounds that it represents not only the play as it was actually performed during Shakespeare's lifetime (whereas the First Quarto is a pirated and garbled version and the Second Quarto is Shakespeare's earliest draft) but also Shakespeare's own revisions in the dozen or so years the play was in the active repertoire of his company. Yet the most recent (and extravagant) production of the play, Kenneth Branagh's film version, returns to the custom of conflating texts, presenting a completely combined form of the Second Quarto with the First Folio (see Chapter 7).

DIFFERENT TEXTS

Until recently most modern editions of *Hamlet* were conflations of the first three published editions: the First Quarto (Q1, 1603), the Second Quarto (Q2, 1604), and the First Folio (F, 1623). Thus the New Arden edition (edited by H. Jenkins, 1982, soon to be replaced by *Arden Three*, edited by Neil Taylor and Ann Thompson) presents Horatio's account, on the ramparts of the castle in Act I, scene i of the danger posed to Denmark by the young prince of Norway:

> Now, sir, young Fortinbras,
> Of unimproved mettle, hot and full,
> Hath in the skirts of Norway here and there
> Shark'd up a list of lawless resolutes
> For food and diet to some enterprise
> That hath a stomach in 't, which is no other,
> As it doth well appear unto our state,
> But to recover of us by strong hand
> And terms compulsatory those foresaid lands
> So by his father lost. And this, I take it,
> Is the main motive of our preparations,
> The source of this our watch, and the chief head
> Of this post haste and rummage in the land. (98–110)

As some indication of this conflation, a textual apparatus is provided, listing variant readings and their sources:

101. lawless] Q2, Q1; Landlesse F. 104. As] Q2; And F. 106. compulsatory] Q2; Compulsative F. 110. rummage] Q2 (Romadge), F (Romage).

The first entry is the preferred reading, "lawless," with its source, here both Q2 and Q1; then the variant "Landlesse" from F. The editor thus has chosen to follow the shared reading of the two earlier editions; such a choice is based not only on the logic of the individual passage and the editor's sense of Shakespeare's style, but also his sense of the relationship among the various editions. So, back in his textual introduction, he tells us:

Of three texts, each of the last two [Q2 and F], though largely substantive, owes something to its predecessor, while the first [Q1], the only wholly independent text, has all the unreliability of a memorial reconstruction. Q2, the one which stands closest to the author, leaves obscure a number of passages which are not represented in the other two at all. . . . On the other hand, F contains passages not in Q2 which are certainly authentic as well as incidental addition almost as certainly spurious. In the matter of variant readings, since F as well as Q1, reflects playhouse deviation from the Shakespearean original, agreement between these two does not authenticate a reading against Q2, and in view of Q2's partial dependence on Q1, agreement between those two, especially in the first act, does not authenticate a reading against F. Moreover, with F also dependent on Q2, agreement even between the two good texts affords no guarantee, and it is obviously possible for all three to be wrong together. (74)

(This last warning justifies modern editors in dismissing the readings of all three early editions and substituting his or her own or someone else's "emendation.") What Jenkins describes here is a logical process that editors of Renaissance texts have followed, in imitation of the great editors of classical texts, such as Richard Bentley and Karl Lachmann, who, confronted with various handwritten manuscripts from antiquity and the Middle Ages, after thorough examination of all the variants, line by line and word by word, drew up a *stemma codicum*, or "family tree of manuscripts," showing which was copied from which and therefore which had precedence.

Thus the editorial process is circular. First, one examines all the different manuscripts or early published editions, noting their variants; then one decides how these texts are related; finally, one comes back to the individual passages and judges each on its own merits. Jenkins, having decided that Q2 is "closest to the author" and Q1 is only a "memorial reconstruction" (i.e., what could be pieced together from memory of one or more performances by one or more actors or members of the audience who had no access to a written text), will on principle follow Q2 when it differs from F, which he regards as "corrupted" by actors' interpolations and other elements alien to the author's original intentions. Since our intention is always to consider the play as a text meant for performance, we might not have so clear a notion of corruption. If we had to choose between two impossibly accurate texts, would we rather have Shakespeare's original autograph copy or a record of an actual performance at the Globe Theatre in 1603 or 1604, or even later?

Some editors believe we have very close to both: that Q2 was set from Shakespeare's "foul papers" (i.e., his own handwritten original, in which he had added, deleted, and changed lines) and that F was set from the Globe's promptbook (the text referred to in production). Editors more recent than Jenkins, however, have different editorial tendencies. They are more interested in production and try to avoid conflation. For instance, G. R. Hibbard explains his procedures for the new Oxford edition (1987):

In keeping with the hypothesis that F *Hamlet* is based on Shakespeare's fair copy and not, as many recent editors and textual critics have argued, on an annotated copy of Q2 or a manuscript that had been compared with Q2, F is used as the control text for the present edition. (131)

The implication is that changes between Q2 and F might represent Shakespeare's own revisions; Q2 is then the rough draft and F the final version refined in performance. Therefore, Hibbard prints *landless* from F in 98 (where Jenkins prints *lawless* from Q2) and explains that it is the rarer word; when it occurs elsewhere, in *King John*, it is used of a character remarkably like Fortinbras. The principle of *difficilior lectio* is basic to textual criticism: the rarer, more precise word is often changed by an insouciant copyist or typesetter into a more common, less appropriate word, a process that results in a weaker, more homogenized text.

All of this reasoning might seem of limited importance if the variations are only of the scope *lawless/landless* and *compulsatory/compulsative*, but there are differences of much larger and more significant dimension. For instance, directly after the passage quoted above (Horatio's account in Act I, scene i) F breaks off and does not resume until eighteen lines later in the Q2 text. What is missing from F is this: Bernardo confirms what Horatio has said so far, relating it all to the previous appearance of the Ghost; then, before the Ghost appears again, Horatio offers a historical analogy:

> A mote it is to trouble the mind's eye.
> In the most high and palmy state of Rome,
> A little ere the mightiest Julius fell.
> The graves stood tenantless and the sheeted dead
> Did squeak and gibber in the Roman streets;
> As stars with trains of fire and dews of blood,
> Disasters in the sun; and the moist star,
> Upon whose influence Neptune's empire stands,
> Was sick almost to doomsday with eclipse.
> And even the like precurse of fear'd events,
> As harbingers preceding still the fates
> And prologue to the omen coming on,
> Have heaven and earth together demonstrated
> Unto our climatures and countrymen. (115–28)

Hibbard puts these lines and others found in Q2 but not in F in an appendix, with this explanation:

These eighteen lines were probably omitted from the text that lies behind F because they do not advance the action in any way. Moreover, if Horatio's speech was, as seems likely, intended to serve as an advertisement for *Julius Caesar*, there would be no point in including it when *Julius Caesar* was not being performed. (355)

On the second point it might be objected that F contains another reference to *Julius Caesar* in Act III, scene 2, lines 99ff., when Hamlet asks Polonius if he had ever acted. His response: "I did enact Julius Caesar. I was kill'd i' th' Capitol. Brutus killed me." The first point is more important. Hibbard, like other editors and critics, would characterize much of what Q2 contains and F lacks as exposition and expansion of an allusive, scholarly nature—what Shakespeare might have originally written (no one doubts their authorship) but later deleted because they did not "play well."

F even lacks the famous "mole of nature" speech that Olivier recites as prologue to his filmed version of *Hamlet*, to focus the audience's attention on

Hamlet's "tragic flaw": "He was a man who could not make up his mind." Horatio has asked about the Danish drinking habits, and Hamlet answers in a long, meditative speech:

> But to my mind, though I am native here
> And to the manner born, it is a custom
> More honour'd in the breach than the observance.
> This heavy-headed revel east and west
> Makes us traduc'd and tax'd of other nations—
> They clepe us drunkards, and with swinish phrase
> Soil our addition; and indeed it takes
> From our achievements, though perform'd at height,
> The pith and marrow of our attribute.
> So, oft it chances with particular men
> That for some vicious mole of nature in them,
> As in their birth, wherein they are not guilty
> (Since nature cannot choose his origin),
> By their o'ergrowth of some complexion,
> Oft breaking down the pales and forts of reason,
> Or by some habit, that too much o'erleavens
> The form of plausive manners—that these men,
> Carrying, I say, the stamp of one defect,
> Being Nature's livery or Fortune's star,
> His virtues else, be they as pure as grace,
> As infinite as man may undergo,
> Shall in the general censure take corruption
> From that particular fault. The dram of evil
> Doth all the noble substance often dout
> To his own scandal. (I.iv.14–38)

Although there are more proximate models for this disquisition on the essentially good man who is morally flawed (Thomas Nashe and Robert Greene have been cited), the ultimate source must be Aristotle, who observed of the tragic hero that he must be "a man who, though not extraordinarily good and just, yet whose misfortune is brought about not by vice or depravity, but rather by some error or frailty" (*Poetics* XIII.3.1453a). The key term is *hamartia*, which is usually translated as "flaw." Shakespeare can be seen, in composing this first of his great tragedies, to meditate here on the nature of the genre, on the qualities of the hero appropriate to its peculiar demands.

If this speech is denied Hamlet, as it is by editors who follow F exclusively, then we miss the hero's defining himself in the leisurely and meditative manner that we have come to think of as particularly his. Again, Hibbard's judgment is that the lines "slow the action down." The contrast between Q2 and F then becomes the classic distinction between the study and the playhouse. Shakespeare developed the character of Hamlet—his brooding melancholy— and the oppressive atmosphere surrounding him at great length in his original text, but where this proved to be static and overwrought in production, cuts were made. Most editors agree that these cuts were accomplished with great subtlety and precision, leaving no break in the sense, no rhetorical or metrical irregularity, and therefore attribute them to Shakespeare.

If we consider the three early versions on a continuum, with Q2 as the most expanded and philosophically developed, then Q1 is the *reductio ad absurdum* of the streamlined stage version. In the scene we have been considering (I.i), Q1 follows F pretty closely. The argument is usually that the actor playing Marcellus might have been the source of this "memorial reconstruction." But even here Q1 breaks off after "some enterprise / That hath a stomach in 't" (96) and skips immediately to the appearance of the Ghost:

> . . . and this (I take it) is the
> Chief head and ground of this our watch.
> But loe, behold, see where it comes again.

"Post-haste and rummage," indeed anything rare and difficult, is dropped or transformed, the gaps then stitched over with awkward and obvious conflations.

In Q1, Hamlet's greatest soliloquy becomes garbled nonsense:

> To be, or not to be, ay there's the point;
> To die, to sleep, is that all? Ay, all.
> No, to sleep, to dream; ay marry, there it goes.
> For in that dream of death, when we awake
> And borne before an everlasting judge,
> From whence no passenger ever returned,
> The undiscovered country, at whose sight
> The happy smile and the accursed damned . . .

And yet even in Q1 there is something to be learned, especially of the logical sequence of scenes and how the action might move more quickly and succinctly. Whereas in Q2 and F Hamlet's "To be or not to be" speech and the nunnery scene follow in Act III, scene i after Claudius has dismissed Rosencrantz and Guildenstern, and placed himself and Polonius behind the arras to eavesdrop, Q1 brings this material forward to Act II, scene ii, to follow directly after Polonius's suggestion of the plan:

> At such a time I'll loose my daughter to him.
> Be you and I behind an arras then,

Mark the encounter. If he love her not,
And be not from his reason fall'n thereon,
Let me be no assistant for a state,
But keep a farm and carters. (162–67)

It has been argued either that Q1 represents the original sequence of action, which was later altered with the expansion of the players' arrival, or that Q1, based only on memory, reflects the confusion of two separate encounters between Hamlet and Polonius. In the first, Hamlet enters reading a book, and when Polonius attempts to engage him in conversation, he abuses the old man as a "fishmonger" (i.e., pander to his own daughter). In the second, Polonius is hidden and Hamlet enters soliloquizing. Then it is Ophelia who is reading a book. There is much awkwardness in the staging of the Q2/F text. With Polonius and Claudius concealed on stage and Ophelia loitering nearby, the high seriousness of "To be and not to be" is compromised. Olivier, in his filmed version, took Hamlet to the ramparts again to recite this speech—his "bare bodkin" then falls over the wall precipitously into the raging sea below—and made Hamlet aware of Claudius's and Polonius's presence in the nunnery scene. He sees their feet beneath the arras, so his abuse of Ophelia is for their benefit; at the end, as she lies sobbing, he silently slips back and kisses her hair (that grotesquely coarse set of blonde braids Jean Simmons was encumbered with).

Two further changes between Q1 and Q2/F involve essential aspects of theme and character. In Q1, a scene is interpolated just before Hamlet's return from England at the end of Act IV. In Q1 Horatio delivers to Gertrude the news of Hamlet's return and the miscarrying of the king's plot to have him murdered. She promises to help her son against her husband, just as, in Q1, she had offered her support earlier, in the closet scene:

[I] will conceal, consent and do my best
What strategem soe'er thou shalt devise.

This makes of Gertrude a more sympathetic figure. (One might recall here that Olivier takes two occasions to effect the same change, though without adding lines. When Gertrude enters the court with Claudius after the closet scene, she distances herself from him. In the dueling scene at the end, she drinks the poisoned cup knowingly, to protect her son.) Some feminist critics have wondered what forces were at work to change her in this way, or, more disturbing, if she were this way to start, why is she more ambiguous and ambivalent in Q2 and F? One suggestion is that "the change in Gertrude's character owes much, if not everything, to the reporter's recollection of Thomas

Kyd's *The Spanish Tragedy*" (Hibbard 86). In that play Bel-Imperia tells Hieronimo:

> ... I will consent, conceal
> And ought that may effect for thine avail,
> Join with thee to revenge Horatio's death.

To which Hieronimo responds:

> On then, whatsoever I devise. ... (IV.1.46–49)

The relation between these two plays is studied in more detail in Chapter 3,
but here it need only be observed that *The Spanish Tragedy* represents revenge
in a rather straightforward manner: the ghost is an observer as the hero pursues his vengeance; those in whom he confides rally to his support. In yet another crucial difference between Q1 and Q2/F we might see further evidence
that the reporters of Q1 have forced Shakespeare's play into assimilation with
Kyd's. One critic has argued:

Q1 reverses . . . the theme of Hamlet's disenchantment with chivalric ideals and heroic
action. It achieves this thematic shift mostly through extensive cuts of material that appears in F. The result . . . is that the Q1 text affirms the ethics of the postfeudal honor
culture, especially the value of heroic individualism, whereas the F text shows Hamlet
accepting the newer Protestant ethic by subordinating his individual will to divine
providence. (Lull in Clayton 137)

No difference could be more radical: does Hamlet believe that he controls his
own destiny or that divine providence controls events? Q1 eliminates his meditation on "the fall of a sparrow":

We defy augury. There's a special providence in the fall of a sparrow. If it be now, 'tis
not to come. If it be not to come, it will be now. If it be not now, yet it will come. The
readiness is all. Since no man knows aught of what he leaves, what is't to leave betimes? Let be. (V.ii.165–170)

Even between Q2 and F there is a reflection of this difference. In F, Hamlet
seems more intent on revenge; in Q2, honor motivates him. In F, Hamlet announces to Horatio at Act V, scene i, lines 75–80 his intention to apologize to
Laertes, but in Q2 a messenger appears at Act V, scene i, line 194, to ask Hamlet, at the queen's request, to "use some gentle entertainment to Laertes." F
lacks the soliloquy, "How all occasions do inform against me" (IV.iv.32–66),
which defines honor, and adds lines in Act V, scene ii that stress necessity

(Westline in Kastan). The Cambridge editor argues that Shakespeare has revised: F, representing his later conception, shows Hamlet's "submission to the guidance of heaven," whereas Q2 shows his concern with the secular demands of honor.

All of our considerations must begin and end with the three texts we have of *Hamlet*. It is to some extent the very process of their conflation in editions and performances that has created our notion of Hamlet's indecision and self-contradiction. The evolution of the text and character shows Shakespeare's consistent concern with the nature of the tragic hero: to what extent does he accept responsibility for his actions and their significance? Is the crucial tragic moment when the hero says of his situation and his character: "The gods made me do it but the deed was mine"?

DIFFERENT EDITIONS

The three major editions available suggest in their sequence the tremendous progress made during the 1980s in understanding the relations among the three earliest editions and their independent values.

The Arden Edition (1982), edited by H. Jenkins, is conflated. It constructs a *Hamlet* out of all available evidence, with no attempt to reconstruct the play at any particular stage of its development. The *Cambridge Shakespeare: Hamlet* (1985), edited by P. Edwards, is an eclectic edition. Edwards is convinced that the First Folio represents most clearly Shakespeare's last thoughts on the play, having been taken not from the Globe promptbook but from a transcript of the original "theatre transcript," prepared by Shakespeare for the earliest productions. Thus, Edwards gives essentially the Folio text, "corrected by" comparison with Q1 and Q2, and supplies in brackets all passages that appear only in Q2. The *Oxford Shakespeare: Hamlet* (1987), edited by G. Hibbard, goes even further: here the exclusively Q2 passages are relegated to an appendix.

There are various other editions available, such as *The New Folger Library: Hamlet* (1992), edited by B. Mowat and P. Werstine; *The Pelican Shakespeare: Hamlet* (1970), edited by W. Farnham; and *The Penguin Hamlet* (1980), edited by T.J.B. Spencer. None of these, however, will provide all the information necessary for continued study of the play.

The Riverside Shakespeare (1997), edited by G. Blakemore Evans et al., though a compendium of all the plays and poems, nevertheless offers a critical text and extensive notes and references. So, too, in less admirable form, do the Norton (1997) and Longman (1997) editions of the complete works, edited by Stephen Greenblatt and David Bevington, respectively.

2

CONTEXTS AND SOURCES

For generations scholars introduced students to the background of a work of literature. In those introductions material contemporary with the work, such as wars, revolutions, religious controversies, and scientific advances, were considered. From the 1930s through the 1950s a movement called the New Criticism took hold in the United States, stressing the intrinsic qualities of the work of literature—its structure, vocabulary, and imagery—almost in isolation from any consideration of the period in which it was written. Then, beginning in the late 1960s, primarily under the influence of the brilliant French historian Michel Foucault, who, in a series of revolutionary studies such as *Madness and Civilization: A History of Insanity in the Age of Reason* (1961), *The Order of Things: An Archaeology of the Human Sciences* (1966), and *Discipline and Punish: The Birth of the Prison* (1975), showed that actual historical change comes about as a function of dynamic changes in whole worldviews, critics began once more to see literature as phenomena integrated with and illustrative of social, political, and intellectual developments. The difference between the old background and the New Historicism is that the former looked at events, whereas the latter studies balances and shifts of power—what are often called "discourses." It seems a much more sophisticated approach. We are told, for instance, not that Queen Elizabeth, known to be Spenser's inspiration for *The Fairie Queene* (1590), might also be Shakespeare's reference in Titania, Queen of the Fairies (*A Midsummer Night's Dream*, 1595), but rather that in the collective popular imagination, the exalted figure of the queen was an enticement to oedipal fantasy—hence "Bottom's Dream" of being intimate with Titania. In these meditations contemporary sources such as letters and diaries, medical treatises, and ships' logs are used in tandem with higher literature to reveal patterns of thought that are simultaneously social, political, and psychosexual.

In these new approaches, valuable associations are revealed—or, rather, arbitrary and artificial boundaries between disciplines are broken down. What is usually lost, however, is the important distinction between common thought (often called by the German term *Zeitgeist*, "spirit of the time") and serious intellectual development, "the history of ideas." Such a distinction is essential to *Hamlet*, since Hamlet himself is a serious thinker who distinguishes himself from such pretenders to knowledge as Polonius and such unthinking creatures of sheer motiveless energy as Fortinbras.

In this chapter I have divided the discussion into five sections. The first, Dates and Sources, looks at Shakespeare's actual literary sources and the historical events contemporary with *Hamlet*'s composition. The second, Historical Context, considers such problems as the Elizabethan conception of melancholy and madness—whether mental aberration was thought to be inherent in the individual or rather his response to intolerable institutions outside himself. Then in the third section, Theological Context, I move into more genuinely intellectual material: the tensions between Catholic and Protestant thinking on the human dilemmas so essential to *Hamlet*, for instance, the immortality of the soul, individual freedom, and responsibility, what is worthwhile in this world, and what is to be expected in the next. In the fourth section, Philosophical Context, I situate Hamlet in intellectual history. Finally, I relate the most profound of Hamlet's concerns with those Shakespeare explores in plays of proximate date, both tragedies and comedies.

DATE AND SOURCES

There is an entry in *The Stationers' Register* dated July 26, 1602, made by James Roberts: "A booke called the Revenge of Hamlett Prince [of] Denmark as yt was latelie Acted by the Lord Chamberleyne his servantes" (Chambers, I.408). Actual publication did not occur until 1603, when the First Quarto appeared. Its printer was not Roberts but Valentine Simmes. The Second Quarto, printed by Roberts, appeared in 1604. There is, then, some lapse of time between first performance and first publication. The question arises: how long was the play being performed before Roberts's entry? In 1598 Francis Meres in his *Palladis Tamia* ("footprints or traces of Athena") fails to mention *Hamlet* among the plays on which Shakespeare's reputation was then based; the "tragedies" mentioned are *Richard II*, *Richard III*, *Henry IV*, *King John*, *Titus Andronicus*, and *Romeo and Juliet*.

Gabriel Harvey, in an edition of Chaucer published in 1598, added this note:

The Earl of Essex much commends Albion's *England*. . . . Lord Mountjoy makes the like account of Daniel's piece of the Chronicle. . . . The younger sort takes much delight in Shakespeare's *Venus and Adonis*, but his *Lucrece* and his *Tragedy of Hamlet, Prince of Denmark* have it in them to please the wiser sort. (232)

The earl of Essex was executed on February 25, 1601, after the insurrection he plotted against Queen Elizabeth failed. We can therefore assume that *Hamlet* went into production at the Globe Theatre in 1599 or 1600. *Julius Caesar*, firmly dated in 1599, is referred to several times in *Hamlet*. Horatio quotes from its account of the omens foretelling Caesar's death (I.i.112ff.); Polonius claims to have acted the part of Caesar when he was a university student (III.ii.91ff.).

What then do we make of the diary entry of Philip Henslowe of a single performance of *Hamlet* at Newington Butts in June 1594 (21), or Thomas Lodge's allusion in 1596 to the "ghost which cried so miserably at the Theatre, like an oister-wife, Hamlet, revenge," or, finally, of this account by Thomas Nashe in 1589, of a play named *Hamlet*:

It is a common practice nowadays amongst a sort of shifting companions, that run through every art and thrive by none, to leave the trade of *Noverint*, whereto they were born and busy themselves with the endeavors of art, that could scarcely Latinize their neck-verse if they should have need. Yet English *Seneca* read by candlelight yields many good sentences, as *Blood is a beggar* and so forth; and if you entreat him fair in a frosty morning, he will afford you whole *Hamlets*—I should say handfuls—of tragical speeches. But . . . *Seneca*, let blood line by line and page by page, at length must needs die to our stage; which makes his famished followers to imitate the Kid in Aesop who, enamoured with the Fox's newfangles, forsook all hopes of life to leap into a new occupation, and these men, renouncing all possibilities of credit or estimation, to intermeddle with Italian translations. (vol. 3, 315–16)

It is clear that Shakespeare's play of *Hamlet* in 1599–1600 was not the first play of that name. Ten years earlier, another *Hamlet*, by another playwright, was making an impression, especially with its ghost demanding revenge. This earlier play, which has not survived, is referred to as the *Ur-Hamlet*, meaning "the archetype or precursor of Shakespeare's *Hamlet*." From the remarks of Nashe, we might assume that its author was Thomas Kyd ("the kid in Aesop"), whose father was a scribe (*Noverint* is the way some legal documents begin: "Let them know that . . .") and whose play *The Spanish Tragedy* has survived. It was printed in 1592, and Kyd died in 1594. If he wrote the *Ur-Hamlet*, then it was probably earlier, as can also be argued from a comparison of the two works.

The Spanish Tragedy bears a remarkable resemblance to *Hamlet* in plot, theme, and incidental action. There are even some verbal echoes, though generally Kyd's verse reads more like Peter Quince's in the satirical "Pyramus and Thisbe" of *A Midsummer Night's Dream* than anything in straightforward Shakespeare. If we examine some of these similarities in detail, we can see the distance between Shakespeare and his sources. G. Bullough determines no fewer than twenty coincidences between *Hamlet* and *The Spanish Tragedy* (I have slightly altered the wording of his categories):

1. A ghost demands revenge.
2. A secret crime is revealed, but verification is required.
3. An oath is taken on the cross of a sword hilt.
4. The avenger falls into doubts, which are then removed.
5. The avenger pretends madness; then a woman actually does go mad.
6. The revenge is delayed, and the revenger reproaches himself.
7. There is contrast between the tardy avenger and another more active and immediate.
8. The avenger contemplates suicide.
9. He uses dissimulation, as do his enemies.
10. The woman loved by the son is manipulated and repressed by her father and brother.
11. The avenger discusses the art of the theatre.
12. A play within the play is presented at a decisive moment.
13. The catastrophe occurs during an alleged entertainment.
14. Both have a character named Horatio, who is a faithful friend.
15. Hamlet knows in the closet scene that the ghost comes to chide him; Hieronimo takes Bazulto to be his son's ghost come to chide him.
16. Hieronimo pretends a reconciliation with his enemy Lorenzo; Hamlet offers Laertes a sincere reconciliation, which Laertes only pretends to accept.
17. A spy is sent to watch the lovers.
18. A brother hates his sister's lover and kills him treacherously.
19. A woman dies by suicide.
20. There are conflicts between two kingdoms, attended by ambassadors, intrigue, crime, and hypocrisy.

Clearly most of these circumstantial similarities are related to the central plot: both plays trace the path to vengeance, through the vicissitudes in the avenger's attitude and the chance events that delay or facilitate his mission. We can always appreciate the conventions of a popular art form better in its mediocre examples than in its masterpiece. Thus the mechanics of the revenge tragedy are clearer in *The Spanish Tragedy* than in *Hamlet*. We can trace the genre forward into the Jacobean period with such plays—more estimable than Kyd's and only slightly less than Shakespeare's—as John Webster's *The Duchess of Malfi* and Cyril Tourneur's *The Revenger's Tragedy*. The basic plot persists into nineteenth-century opera: Verdi's *La Forza del Destino* has very much the same concerns. At the heart of these plays is the obsession with honor. A man loses his honor if he fails to uphold his obligations to friends and family; a woman loses her honor if she is unchaste or allies herself with a man socially inferior to her. The action often takes place in Spain, where honor combines with religion to become an obsession, and masculine pride is focused on the family. In *The Spanish Tragedy* Bel-Imperia had fallen in love with Don Andrea, whom her father, the duke of Castile, and her brother, Lorenzo, considered an unworthy match. Andrea is killed in battle by the Portuguese Prince Balthazar, who is then captured by the Spanish. Lorenzo decides that Balthazar is worthy of his sister, but she has in the meantime fallen in love with Andrea's friend Horatio; Lorenzo and Balthazar then kill Horatio. Horatio's father becomes the avenger and works finally through to wholesale vengeance on both royal families. Watching all this is the ghost of Andrea and the personification Revenge.

In this circumstance, we see also something essential to *Hamlet*: the use of theatre as metaphor, or what has come to be called the metatheatrical effect. Hamlet rewrites a play about an actual murder, to make its circumstances closer to those surrounding his father's murder by his uncle Claudius; through this use of theatre he can "catch the conscience of the king." In *The Spanish Tragedy* Hieronimo acts as the presenter of a masque; we might compare Prospero in *The Tempest*. He assigns parts in a play he has written to Bel-Imperia, Lorenzo, and Balthazar. In this play within the play, the part assigned to Lorenzo is that of Erasto, a knight of Rhodes, beloved by Perseda, played by Bel-Imperia. Balthazar is assigned the part of Soliman, sultan of Turkey, who has his henchman Bashaw kill Erasto, so he can win the love of Perseda. Hieronimo himself takes the part of Bashaw and actually kills Lorenzo on stage. Bel-Imperia then actually kills Balthazar on stage, and then herself. In the melee that follows, Hieronimo also manages to kill the father of Lorenzo and Bel-Imperia, who has been in the audience, and finally himself. Andrea's ghost is satisfied with these proceedings, but Revenge assures him that in addition the villains will be punished eternally in hell and that the virtuous will be reunited in bliss (presumably an extracorporeal *menage à trois*, since both Horatio and Andrea loved Bel-Imperia).

In *Hamlet* we see two theatrical events: the play within the play, where Claudius sees a reenactment of his murder of Hamlet's father, and then the catastrophe of the fencing match, where a seemingly innocent duel is turned into a murderous frenzy by the addition of poison to cup and sword. After Laertes, Claudius, and Gertrude have died and Hamlet lies dying in Horatio's arms, he calls attention to this convention:

> You that look pale and tremble at this chance,
> That are but mutes or audience to this act,
> Had I but time—as this fell sergeant Death,
> Is strict in his arrest—O, I could tell you—
> But let it be. Horatio, I am dead,
> Thou livest. Report me and my cause aright
> To the unsatisfied. (V.ii.339–45)

The members of the court, gathered to watch the duel, are combined with us the audience in the theatre as but extra players ("mutes") or witnesses to the disaster, perhaps like the chorus of citizens in Greek tragedy, who can only watch and lament as the members of the royal family kill each other.

In *The Spanish Tragedy* the play itself is being watched as a play by the ghost of Andrea, presented to him as spectacle by Revenge, and within that there is the play within the play presented by Hieronimo for the royal families of Spain and Portugal. This turns out to be the slaughter of their children. Such forceful comparison of life to the theatre is not just a device for Shakespeare and his contemporaries but part of their worldview. Shakespeare constantly calls attention to the congruence of the Globe Theatre with the globe of the world:

> And like the baseless fabric of this vision,
> The cloud-capped towers, the gorgeous palaces,
> The solemn temples, the great globe itself—
> Yea, all which it inherit—shall dissolve
> And like this insubstantial pageant faded,
> Leave not a rack behind. (*Tempest* IV.i.151–152)

. . . this goodly frame the earth seems to me a sterile promontory, this most excellent canopy the air, look you, this brave o'erhanging firmament, this majestical roof fretted with golden fire, why, it appeareth nothing to me but a foul and pestilent congregation of vapours. (*Hamlet* II.ii.298–302)

The actor delivering Hamlet's lines would have stood far forward on the thrust stage of the Globe Theatre, pointing up to the rafters, which were painted to look like the sky, "fretted" with stars. If "all the world's a stage, / And all the men and women merely players" (*As You Like It*, II.vii.139–40), then the audience at the theatre is encouraged both to see themselves as witnesses to momentous events and also to see those momentous events as but the entertainment of an afternoon. In other words, by forcing the metaphor of life as theatrical art, the playwright dissolves the difference between audience and actors and forces us to see ourselves as manipulated by forces beyond our control, just as the actors can only play their parts as written by the playwright.

In comparing *The Spanish Tragedy* with *Hamlet*, we see that what is a creaking convention in the one becomes a profound philosophical speculation in the other. I give one more example of this kind of similarity and difference. Kyd has a habit of playing with rhetorical devices. This, like his fondness for ghosts and personified abstractions, probably derives from the Roman playwright Seneca, whom almost all Elizabethan playwrights imitated to some degree. In Latin one can turn a phrase simply by changing the form of a word. Kyd uses Latin phrases throughout *The Spanish Tragedy* and at one point puts a whole speech for his revenger into Latin (II.iv.131–44), a pastiche of lines from ancient authors stitched together with his own phrases. Hieronimo asks for death or oblivion:

> Aut, si qui faciunt animis oblivia, succos
> Praebeat; ipse metam magnum quaecunque per orbem
> Gramina Sol pulchras effert in lumina oras;
> Ipse bibam quicquid meditatur saga veneni. (133–36)

> Or, if there be juices which can bring forth forgetfulness,
> Let her offer it; I myself shall gather throughout the wide world
> Those grasses which the Sun brings forth into beautiful realms of light,
> I myself shall drink whatever poison the witch administers.

In Latin the subject of the verb is implied in the ending of the verb, so there is no need of a personal pronoun. *Metam* means "I shall gather," *bibam* "I shall drink." When *ipse* is added, it is an intensifier, or something like a demonstrative: "I myself [as distinguished from this other person I have just mentioned] shall gather . . . I myself shall drink." Throughout the English portions of *The Spanish Tragedy*, Kyd plays with the English equivalent "myself" and related forms. The king of Spain uses the royal first-person plural in a way that magnifies and separates out his power from his person: "Our selfe will exempt the place" (III.xii.99), referring to Hieronimo's strange behavior. Hieronimo apostrophizes Balthazar:

> Woe to thy birth, thy body and thy soul,
> Thy cursed father, and thy conquered selfe. (III.vii.63–64)

The intrusion of the epithet "conquered" between "thy" and "selfe" hypostatizes "self," makes it seem to have an existence separate and apart from Balthazar himself. So, too, in Hieronimo's confusion of self and other in his interview with Bazulto:

> Heere, take my hand-kercher and wipe thine eies
> Whiles wretched I, in thy mishaps may see,
> The lively portrait of my dying selfe,
> O no, not this, Horatio this was thine. (III.xiii.88–91)

He has just confused Bazulto, who comes to petition him to avenge his son's murder, with his own murdered son, whose bloody handkerchief he carries as an inducement to his own vengeance.

Kyd, in his use of soliloquies and these circumlocutions of "self," calls attention to the extremity of Hieronimo's situation. He is alienated from the court because of his grief, and he slips into madness when he delays his vengeance. In Shakespeare's *Hamlet*, there is a more profound philosophical development to both of these devices, but it follows the same lines as those laid down by Kyd. When Hamlet first meets Horatio, he exclaims: "Horatio, or I do forget myself" (I.ii.101). This can mean one or a combination of three slightly different things: (1) the idiom "I forget myself" means little more than "I am absent-minded"; (2) "I am as likely to forget you as forget myself"; (3) "In forgetting you I forget my *self*—that essence of myself which is externalized in you." This last reading gains support from the later speech to Horatio, in which Hamlet analyzes their friendship:

> Since my dear soul was mistress of her choice,
> And could of men distinguish her election,
> Sh'ath seal'd thee for herself; for thou
> Art one, in suff'ring all, that suffers nothing. (III.ii.63–66)

Here the ambiguity is again between "herself" and her *self*, but also in the sense of "for," which can mean either "for the benefit of" or "as, in place of." Hamlet says both: "My soul has claimed Horatio as her own," and "My soul has broken down all barriers between herself and Horatio and Horatio now is my soul—that external, separate part of myself." The rhetoric creates a philosophical distinction; the grammar hypostatizes the sense of what is unique in the individual. Also in this passage, as often in Kyd, there is mention of both "soul" and "self," as if some attempt were being made to develop a new language to express in purely human terms the existence of a person's essence on the analogy of the theological term "soul," that separable, immortal aspect of the human being. (The insistence on the soul's being feminine comes again from the Latin, where *anima* is a feminine noun; the same is true for the Greek, *psyche*, and the German, *Seele*.) Nothing could come closer to the heart of *Hamlet* than this attempt: his early soliloquies focus on the possibility of the survival of the soul to suffer after death. From the graveyard scene on, there is no suggestion of immortality, except that which Horatio will give him in telling his tale. One aspect of the development in Hamlet's character is then from the Christian belief in the immortality of the soul—and thus the potentiality for infinite punishment—to the humanistic position that the individual exists in the dimension of his own thinking about himself, how he relates to others (like or unlike, friend or foe, etc.), and how he justifies his actions. Hamlet questions, never accepting conventional wisdom. He specifically questions playing the role of the avenger, a convention established in such plays as Kyd's *The Spanish Tragedy.*

The ultimate source for Shakespeare and the author of the *Ur-Hamlet* is Saxo Grammaticus's *Historiae Danicae,* written in Latin at the end of the twelfth century but not printed until 1514, after which there were several editions and a Danish translation in 1575. The story of Amleth, though in prose, reads like an epic, with its focus clearly on the virtues of its hero, following him from adventure to adventure, but balancing these in clearly marked thematic contrasts.

Rorik is the king of Denmark and marries his daughter, Gerutha, off to Horwendil, son of Gerwendil. The family has some claim to rule in Jutland, but Horwendil has also distinguished himself by killing Kroll, king of Norway, in a duel. Horwendil and Gerutha have a son, Amleth; Horwendil has a brother, Feng, presumably younger. What follows is remarkably like the story of Pelops's two sons, Atreus and Thyestes: brothers dispute the throne and with it is identified the possession of the same woman. Saxo seems to reflect on the biblical story of Cain and Abel, stressing Feng's jealousy of Horwendil's great accomplishments, crowned by his marriage to the king's daughter. Saxo expresses horror that "the same hands caress the brother's wife as killed the brother." This profound insight into the intimacy of the crimes of fratricide and incest persists throughout. (Shakespeare's Hamlet captures it in his opening line, "More than kin and less that kind.") Feng kills his brother and marries the widow, and so Amleth is raised aware of his father's murder and therefore fearful for his own life. He thus pretends madness, wallowing in filth, wearing ragged clothes, and idly occupying himself with strange tasks, such as carving hooked darts with which he says he will avenge his father's murder. Saxo then emphasizes the prince's blighted youth; he has been cheated of his heritage, and the contrast between his golden expectations and his present squalor arouses pity. He is thought mad; any young man of his lineage who does not distinguish himself must be degenerate. Indeed Saxo makes constant reference to what is natural and what is unnatural. We might recall how consistent Shakespeare's references are to nature, especially in the opening scenes of *Hamlet.* His first soliloquy has as its central concept what is "rank and gross in nature."

Amleth's feigned madness conceals great intelligence and integrity. (Saxo even makes the analogy between the accomplishments of his craftsmanship and the brilliance of his mind.) Whenever he makes outrageous propositions, they are based on actual truths, though metaphorically expressed. He says the keel of a ship is a knife that cuts ham, and so it does if the sea is seen as a ham. The ocean is a mill that grinds meal (i.e., the sand). These are kennings—those tropes characteristic of the medieval verse sagas, wherein a ship is "the horse of the sea." An essential insight is hidden under analogy. It is also a feature of dreams and oracles. Lucius Junius Brutus, who was to bring down the Tarquin kings of Rome, feigned madness; *Brutus* means "stupid." When he accompanied some young Tarquins to the oracle at Delphi, where they were told that he would rule Rome who should first kiss his mother upon his return, only Brutus knew to kiss his native ground: the earth is mother of all. (Shakespeare shows fascination with Brutus throughout this period, invoking his feigned madness also in *The Rape of Lucrece*, *Julius Caesar*, and *Henry V*.)

Feng's suspicions are aroused, and he causes Amleth to be "tested": some young men of the court lead him to a place in the forest where he discovers a young girl he has known since childhood. The idea is that if he really is stupid, he will do nothing, but if he is normal he will "yield to wantonness." As if to show the mettle of his hero, Saxo has Amleth seduce the young woman but bind her by oath to deny it. Back at court, he then admits what he has done, but she contradicts him, so again he seems the fool. This is a strange prefiguration of the closet scene in *Hamlet*, where Hamlet makes his mother swear *not* to tell that he is mad (III.iv), as also he has caused his companions on the ramparts *not* to tell (I.v); one usually swears positive oaths.

Saxo makes Gerutha, as well as Amleth, unaware that their interview is to be overheard by a hidden courtier; this is the second test, like the first in its assimilation of intimacy with the woman and revelation of the truth. The courtier (Polonius in *Hamlet*) hides in the straw of the bed, but Amleth sniffs him out, stabs him, dismembers his body, and flushes the pieces down the sewer to be eaten by swine. He then upbraids his mother in terms much like Hamlet's of Gertrude:

Most infamous of women! dost thou seek with such lying lamentations to hide thy most heavy guilt? Wantoning like a harlot, thou hast entered a wicked and abominable state of wedlock, embracing with incestuous bosom thy husband's slayer, and wheedling with filthy lures of blandishment him who had slain the father of thy son. (Bullough 66)

Here we might pause to consider the depiction of women in Saxo. Some indication that his attitude toward women is complex comes early in the Amleth narrative. Amleth's father, Horwendil, after killing King Kroll of Norway, pursues his sister, Sele, and kills her: "she was a skilled warrior and experienced in piracy." Later, after Amleth first perceives the truth, we hear that the king of Britain is a bastard, the son of a slave who had seduced his mother. The Scottish Queen Hermutrude kills her unsuccessful suitors, but seduces Amleth through an exchange of letters much like that whereby Amleth saves himself in Britain and causes his faithless companions to be killed (Rosencrantz and Guildenstern in *Hamlet*). After Amleth marries Hermutrude, he returns with her to Britain, where he already has a wife, who responds to his bigamy by saying, "It would be unworthy of me to hate you as an adulterer more than I loved you as husband." Finally, after Amleth has been killed by Wiglek, king of Denmark, following Rorik's death, Hermutrude, though she had protested she would not outlive her husband, immediately marries his killer. (This episode obviously lies behind the play within the play in *Hamlet*.)

Women then play a variety of active roles in the story; its thematic center is their faithfulness. In Amleth's address to the people after his murder of Feng, he asks pity for himself and for his mother, Gerutha:

Pity also my stricken mother, and rejoice with me that the infamy of her who was once your queen is quenched. For this weak woman had to bear a two-fold weight of ignominy, embracing one who was her husband's brother and murderer. (Bullough 72)

Epic traditionally refuses to moralize, especially when it comes to women. The old men of Troy lament in the *Iliad* the coming of Helen, but remember from their youth what power love has and therefore do not blame Paris. It is taken for granted that a woman is worth fighting for and that any shame she might incur can be obliterated if her champion is victorious. In the *Odyssey* Menelaus takes Helen back home, and there she is the perfect hostess, mixing magical herbs into a potion of forgetfulness for the warriors returning to Greece. All this points toward the recognition that Saxo is "precourtly." He writes before the troubadours in the south of France—and then the prose romancers in the north—established the courtly love tradition, wherein the lady is set apart from the active world of men and worshipped as an idol of perfection; any woman falling short of this ideal is a whore. We find an example of this split in *The Spanish Tragedy*, where Bel-Imperia is chaste and faithful in fact, but in scandalous report she is profligate and ungovernable. So, too, of course, in *Hamlet*: Gertrude has had "Rebellious hell . . . mutine in [her] matron's bones," but Ophelia is pure. (Notoriously Hamlet confuses the two, telling Ophelia, "Get thee to a nunnery," which in Elizabethan slang could mean a whorehouse.) Saxo is innocent of all this. For him, women can be as varied as men, their character determined by circumstance, which in fact is his conclusion of Amleth's own career:

Had fortune been as kind to him as nature, he would have equalled the gods in glory. (Bullough 79)

Do we see here the pattern for Fortinbras's eulogy of Hamlet:

> For he was likely, had he been put on,
> To have proved most royal. (V.ii.402–403)

There is a possible secondary source for both the author of the *Ur-Hamlet* and for Shakespeare: a collection of stories in French, *Histoires Tragiques*, written by François de Belleforest, and published seven times between 1564 and 1582 but not translated into English until 1608. The very name of the collection has resonance with the title pages of the First and Second Quartos of *Hamlet: The Tragical Historie of Hamlet, Prince of Denmark.* Belleforest does not translate Saxo straightforwardly but rather presents the tale, augments and amends it, and comments on it at great length. These comments are otiose, inelegant, and absurd, falling into two main categories: apologies for the tale's being set in pre-Christian and in precourtly times. In his opening chapter, he opines that "long before the kingdom of Denmark received the faith of Jesus Christ, . . . if ther were sometime a good prince or king among them who . . . would addict himselfe to vertue, and use courtesie," he would be destroyed. Not only does this moralizing tendency set Belleforest against Saxo, but it also specifies what this adapter looks for and does not find there: the strictures of the courtly love tradition. This shows both in the constant terminology—"courtesie . . . courteous . . . courtesie" (Bullough 87–89)—and also in the misogyny that pervades his entire narrative. Although the major differences in details of the plot might be confined to three, the tone is overwhelmingly different. Belleforest insists that Fengon had already committed adultery with Hamlet's mother before he murdered her husband; he also suggests that Geruthe might have inspired the crime and that Hamlet's communication with the spirit world (unquestioned in Saxo) derives from his melancholy, which is a consequence of his mother's perfidy. (In neither Saxo nor Belleforest is Hamlet visited by a ghost; Hieronimo in *The Spanish Tragedy* is not visited by a ghost—though he thinks he is—but he does go mad under the pressure to pursue vengeance. The ghost is first attested in the *Ur-Hamlet*.)

I have already noted that the guilt of Gertrude is disputed among the different early editions. In the First Quarto, she immediately responds to Hamlet's exposure of her guilt in the closet scene. In fact, she echoes the words of Bel-Imperia when Hieronimo invokes her participation in his plan for vengeance in *The Spanish Tragedy*:

> Hamlet, I vow by that maiesty,
> That know as our thoughts, and looks into our hearts,
> I will conceale, consent and doe my best,
> What strategem so e're thou shalt devise. (G3recto–G3verso)

> I will consent, conceale,
> And ought that may effect for thine availe,
> Joyne with thee to revenge Horatioes death. (IV.i.46–48)

It is clearer and more straightforward to present Gertrude as an unwitting accomplice, indeed a victim, of Claudius's plot to murder and usurp. Shakespeare's Gertrude in the Second Quarto and Folio versions is more complex. This is both dramatic sophistication and Shakespeare's own career-long response to the courtly love tradition. In the comedies he consistently opposes the naive young male lover who wants to idolize his beloved with the lady herself, who refuses to be treated in that simplistic, confining manner. The clearest examples are the relations between the sexes in *Much Ado About Nothing* and *As You Like It*. Tragic variations occur in *Romeo and Juliet* and *Othello*. There is a comprehensiveness in Saxo's treatment of women—in Belleforest, a narrow-minded misogyny derived from the courtly love tradition. My suggestion is that Shakespeare's fully developed Gertrude is perhaps a spontaneous reconstruction of the former, although the author of the *Ur-Hamlet* might only have followed the latter.

Critics are divided on the question of how much independent recourse Shakespeare might have had to either Saxo or Belleforest. The best analogy seems to be his use of sources in *Henry IV* and *Henry V*, where his immediate source was a "ramshakle" earlier play, *The Famous Victories of Henry V*, but he had constant reference to the ultimate source Holinshed's *Chronicles* (*The Oxford Shakespeare*, 13).

Various passages in Shakespeare's play have various literary and traditional sources. Several of the most interesting are classical. When Hamlet approaches his mother's bedroom, he admonishes himself:

> Let not
> The soul of Nero enter this firm bosom. (III.iii.384–85)

The Ghost had previously directed him:

Taint not thy mind nor let thy soul contrive
Against thy mother aught. Leave her to heaven. (I.v.85–86)

Nero murdered his mother, Agrippina, so this reference is clear. Further, however, Agrippina is said to have been incestuously involved with her son and to have poisoned her second husband, Claudius, to gain the throne for him (hence, Shakespeare's name for Hamlet's uncle). That marriage itself was incestuous, since she was the daughter of Claudius's brother Germanicus (i.e., his niece). Shakespeare would have known all this from Tacitus's *Annals*. From Virgil's *Aeneid* he would have known the story of the fall of Troy, which is the subject of the First Player's speech (II.ii.446–514). Pyrrhus, the son of Achilles, kills Priam, king of Troy, in front of his queen, Hecuba. Some have seen in this yet another example of vengeance accomplished by son for father—along with Laertes and Fortinbras—since Achilles had died at the hands of Priam's son, Paris. Christopher Marlowe and Thomas Nashe presented their version in *The Tragedie of Dido Queene of Carthage* (1594); in Virgil Dido first falls in love with Aeneas as he tells this story. It should be noted, however, that in putting this speech in the mouth of the First Player, Shakespeare does not parody Marlowe's style. Rather, it is the older, more rhetorical style, closer to that of Kyd.

In another category belong various historical and literary documents that show striking similarity to certain aspects of *Hamlet* and also fix it fascinatingly in its period. Not the least of these is a verse epistle written to James VI of Scotland—later, after the death of Queen Elizabeth in 1603, James I of England—urging him to avenge the murder of his father, Lord Darnley, many years before. The poem was written in Latin at the court of King Henry III of France, and not published until 1875. Elizabeth had James's mother, Mary, queen of Scots, executed in 1586, after the discovery of letters that implicated her in a plot to overthrow Elizabeth. Mary had thrown herself on the mercy of her cousin some years earlier when her third husband, James Hepburn, earl of Bothwell, was driven from Scotland for the murder of Darnley. The ghost of Darnley addresses his son:

I

Came blameless down to you, Ancestral Shades,
Believe no crime of me, unless 'tis wrong
When any husband loves his wife too much.
And thou my wife, dearer to me than breath,
Whose heart so changed against me on behalf
Of a vile rascal pardoned in despite
Of Lords' just anger and the People's wrongs! (Bullough 125)

One must think of the situation in *Hamlet*—one man kills another to gain throne and queen—and, especially, of Hamlet's impression of his dead father's love for his mother:

> so loving of my mother
> That he might not beteem the winds of heaven
> Visit her face too roughly. (I.ii.140–42)

The similarity is variously explained. John Gordon, the author of the letter, must have known his Seneca as well as did Kyd or Shakespeare. (Seneca's *Agamemnon* opens with the ghost of Thyestes appealing for vengeance against the house of Atreus, his brother and murderer.) If the *Ur-Hamlet* was as early as 1587—it is first attested in 1589—Gordon could have seen the analogy. The important point here is the congruence—the mutual influence between plays that treat the lives and deaths of kings and those lives themselves. We know, for instance, that Essex had Shakespeare's *Richard II* performed in London on the eve of his rebellion: a play about usurpation then was thought to have power to put that possibility in the minds of its audience. (We think again of Shakespeare's constant conceit that the Globe is the globe, and vice versa.) Historically there are connections between Scotland and Denmark: Bothwell sought refuge in Denmark and offered to cede the northern islands of Scotland to the Danish king; he was moved then to confinement in Sweden and finally to Zeeland, where he went insane and died in 1578.

In 1585 when James VI was nearly 20 and his mother was a prisoner in England, Queen Elizabeth was disturbed when an embassy arrived in Edinburgh from Denmark ostensibly to demand the return to Danish rule of the isles of Orkney and Shetland, and also to suggest that James should marry a Danish princess. The Queen opposed the proposal but friendly relations were set up between Scotland and Denmark and Scottish ambassadors went over in 1588. The death of Frederick II delayed the match but in June 1589 a retinue sailed to Copenhagen to bring back the bride, who was married to James by proxy on 20 August 1589. Contrary winds however prevented her crossing the North Sea and her ship was in peril and took shelter in Norway. Thither the eager bridegroom sailed, leaving Leith on 22 October 1589. He met Anne at Oslo on 19 November and married her in person four days later. They did not arrive in Scotland until 1 May 1590. (Bullough 18)

In discussions of the passages in *Hamlet* printed in the Second Quarto but missing from the Folio, it has been suggested that Hamlet's long speech beginning, "This heavy-handed revel east and west" (I.iv.16), and going on to compare Danish drunkenness with the "mole of nature" in individual men, was cut in performance before Queen Anne so as not to offend her in reference to her countrymen. On the accession of Christian IV of Denmark, Queen Elizabeth sent as emissary Daniel Rogers, who notes in dispatches the attendance at Elsinore of George Rosenkrantz of Rosenholm, Alex Guildenstern of Lyngbye, and Peter Guildenstern, marshal of Denmark.

Other contemporary texts offer tantalizing similarities with *Hamlet*, but they are of an anecdotal character. In *The St. Albans Chronicle*, a man is visited by his father's ghost, who reports that he was killed by his wife; in *A Warning for Fair Women*, a woman who killed her husband starts up and confesses when she sees a play depicting the same circumstance. Francesco Maria I, duke of Urbino, died suddenly in 1538, and Luigi Gonzaga is accused of having bribed his barber to blow poison dust in his ears.

A literary document of an entirely different nature is the play *Der Bestrafte Brudermord*, or "Fratricide Punished," which was being performed in Germany as early as 1626. It is a remarkable piece of work, proving once again that dramatic material takes on a life of its own once it enters the popular repertory.

The play opens with a prologue spoken by Night, who claims protection of illicit lovers; she is then joined by the three Furies, and they prepare us for vengeance that will be taken on the King Erico and Queen Sigrie of Denmark by Hamlet, son of the dead king. The ghost of the dead king then appears seeking his son, and so on. The action follows that in the First Quarto, with the nunnery scene immediately after the old counselor first suggests it and before the entrance of the players. Bullough offers a precise analysis, following Duthie, to show that *Der Brudermord* has echoes of both the First and Second Quartos (see notes to the text 128–58); there are also similarities, in addition to the prologue speech by a personified abstraction, with *The Spanish Tragedy*. The easiest surmise is thus that this troupe of actors playing *Hamlet* in Germany knew not only different versions of Shakespeare's play but the *Ur-Hamlet* as well. We need not think of actual manuscripts or printed editions in their possession, however, but rather only of their collective memory. Just as the actor taking the part of Marcellus is thought to be responsible for the memorial reconstruction that lies behind the First Quarto, so several actors who had performed various parts of both Shakespeare's *Hamlet* and the *Ur-Hamlet* seem to have collaborated on *Der Brudermord*. This illustrates the after-life of a great play in the theatre, as does a version of the Hamlet story that entered French folklore (Bullough 9–10) illustrate the metamorphosis of high art back into the milieu from which it first emerged.

HISTORICAL CONTEXT

We have already noted that political events contemporary with Shakespeare's *Hamlet* (or the earlier play of that name) may have had some influence on its conception of plot and character, its dialogue and incidental action.

Dynastic marriages, foreign alliances, threats of rebellion, and usurpation all force the fictional courts of Denmark and England in *Hamlet* into comparison with what was actually happening in the final years of Elizabeth's reign. I now take one example of such a political occurrence and use it to open larger issues of religious, psychological, and philosophical background to the play. It is easier for us to appreciate the similarity of precise events—action on stage with historical moments of a political nature—than it is to understand the broader problems and deeper resonances of intellectual history. What were English people thinking at the end of the sixteenth century about God, themselves, and their access to truth?

To bridge the political and intellectual spheres is particularly important in any consideration of Hamlet. He is an intellectual disdainful of, yet inescapably bound up with, the intrigues of the court. Fortunately there has been recent investigation of the extraordinary career of Robert Devereux, second earl of Essex, which illustrates how a historical figure can influence the development of a dramatic character and also how the dramatic character can help us understand the political pressures and intellectual forces of the times. Coddon opens her consideration of "Madness, Subjectivity and Treason in *Hamlet* and Elizabethan Culture" (380–402), with a quotation from a contemporary's account of Essex (381):

It resteth with me in opinion, that ambition thwarted in its career, doth speedily lead on to madness; herein I am strengthened by what I learn of my Lord of Essex, who shifteth from sorrow and repentance to rage and rebellion so suddenly, as well proveth him devoid of good reason or right mind; in my last discourse, he uttered such strange designs that made me hasten forth, and leave his absence. . . . The Queene well knoweth how to humble the haughty spirit. The haughty spirit knoweth not how to yield, and the man's soul seemeth tossed to and fro like the waves of a troubled sea. (Harington 225–26)

What drives men mad? Harington's answer on Essex is "thwarted ambition." In the England of the aging Elizabeth, there was no scope for ambitious young aristocrats. In Hamlet's Denmark, suggestions are made of a similar frustration. Hamlet describes Denmark as a prison to Rosencrantz and Guildenstern, who then attribute his melancholy to ambition, which makes his mind feel captive. Though he denies that suggestion here (II.ii.298ff.), he later confirms it, though perhaps sarcastically: "I lack advancement" (III.ii.320).

Essex's greatest affronts against the queen before his failed rebellion were in crossing courtly boundaries. When in a dispute she boxes his ears, he instinctively moves to draw his sword. (One cannot not think of Achilles about to draw his sword against Agamemnon during their abusive interview at the opening of the *Iliad*.) Then returning from Ireland, where he had usurped certain royal prerogatives, he storms into her bedchamber to discover her *en déshabillé.* Conflating these two moments, we see Hamlet rushing into his mother's bedchamber in Act III, scene iv, his sword still drawn from his aborted attempt to kill Claudius on the landing. Gertrude cries out, "What wilt thou do? Wilt thou murther me? Help, ho!" (21–22). Polonius behind the arras cries out in response, and Hamlet kills him.

It might seem that these are two entirely different types of situations—one involving an insubordinate courtier and the other a distraught son—but in fact deep psychological similarities connect them. Queen Elizabeth claimed she was married to her people, wearing her coronation ring on the wedding finger. As she aged, she began to assume in the popular imagination all the attributes of an overwhelming mother, although she continued to see herself as a beautiful young girl. (When Hamlet in the graveyard speaks to Yorick's skull as if it were a messenger, "Now get you to my lady's chamber and tell her, let her paint an inch thick, to this favour she must come," we think of both Elizabeth, who did wear makeup an inch thick, and Gertrude, since that was the last lady's chamber he was in.) The contradiction between authority and seduction is precisely what Hamlet faces in his mother. He expects her to behave like a mature matron, but she is newly a bride; his response to this double image is complex, to say the least. Montrose has compared a dream recorded by the charlatan Simon Foreman almost contemporary with Shakespeare's *A Mid-summer Night's Dream.* Foreman dreams he enters Queen Elizabeth's bedchamber; Bottom's dream is that he is beloved of Titania, Queen of the Fairies. Intruding upon royal arcana is analogous to defying the taboo of the mother's body. When the weapon drawn is the sword and not the penis, then the oedipal attack takes on even more complex meanings. We should remember that Oedipus himself, in Sophocles' play, has his sword drawn when he enters Iocaste's bedchamber: to strike that part of her body where "he sowed and was sown." Essex vents his frustration and resentment on the queen; she becomes the focus, and in his mind the cause, of all his thwarted ambitions. Hamlet, we shall see, blames his mother for even more: the precisely mortal and physical limitation of his human condition.

In even these cursory remarks on the striking similarity between Essex and Hamlet, I have invoked several models with explanatory potential. The most demanding task is first to distinguish the historically specific from the more modern, but then to see how these mutually explicate each other. In the late sixteenth century, there was a variety of explanations for madness. One is the theory of the bodily humors. Melancholy, which Freud called dementia prae-cox and we call depression, was, as its name implies ("black anger"), attributed to a superflux of black bile (Bright 2). It was also believed that those born under the influence of the planet Saturn have similar characteristics (Burton). We might oppose these "natural" causes to the situational. Young men in love are melancholy, as are those who seek advancement and fail to attain it. Thus in *As You Like It*, the melancholy of Orlando is ridiculed by Rosalind, as is also the melancholy of Jacques by Orlando. In *Hamlet* both causes are suggested but put aside. Polonius keeps insisting that Hamlet's melancholy derives from his unrequited love of Ophelia, but Gertrude insists to Claudius:

> I doubt it is no other but the main,
> His father's death and our o'erhasty marriage. (II.ii.56–57)

We have already seen where he contradicts Rosencrantz's and Guildenstern's attribution of his malaise to thwarted ambition. Recent critics have suggested that the difficulty of Shakespeare's play is in part due to its aporetic nature: propositions are posed and negated, but little of a purely positive nature emerges (see Wofford 389, notes 8, 9). They think that our modern notions of subjectivity were not yet developed in late-sixteenth-century texts, so we look in vain there for the sort of precision we have been accustomed to find in the modern novel, for instance, or, more obviously, the psychoanalytic case study. It might prove useful then to see the character of Hamlet as problematic primarily because Shakespeare rejected contemporary explanations for disaffection from the world, but nevertheless presented a convincing portrait of its ravages on individual character.

Studies of other parts of the Shakespeare canon are also helpful here. Joel Fineman has found in the sonnets the representation of a crisis in poetry itself and its ability to represent the individual's consciousness of himself: poetry can misrepresent reality, and therefore its truth value lies not in objective but rather in subjective views of the world. The lyric persona then confronts its own hallucinatory worldview, and our sense of its authority comes from an appreciation of how it reconciles contradictions. What, then, of the dramatic persona? We must read Hamlet against *Hamlet*; we have here not only his impression of the world and his place in it, but also the other characters' impressions of him. The dynamic of this relationship is best brought out on stage. In the recent Ralph Fiennes *Hamlet*, we ask different questions. Rather than the traditional, "What's wrong with Hamlet?" this production demands, "What's wrong with Hamlet's world?" It is in the very nature of drama to call attention to human experience: things happen, and characters respond. If they meditate philosophically or psychologically, this is closely related to the action. Indeed, if it is not—if such meditations break forth from the moorings of the action and float freely in the stratosphere of pure speculation—we feel this break "is from the purpose of playing."

Another approach to Hamlet's madness, which is also well grounded in history, is suggested by W. Benjamin's critique of seventeenth-century German

Trauerspiel, a dramatic form related to tragedy but significantly different. I shall say more about his argument in the next section; here I mention it only as a correction to critics who say Hamlet's madness is inadequately explained because modern subjectivity is incompletely developed in late-sixteenth-century texts. Benjamin says, on the contrary, that Shakespeare in *Hamlet*, like the authors of *Trauerspiel*, is not interested in the tragic effect, which he defines as the hero's transcendence of myth—that moment in which the hero both accepts and contradicts the power the gods have over him, thus rising above the level of normal human experience and, paradoxically, beyond the intensity of divine existence: gods can never define themselves in conflict as tragic heroes do because they face no conflict; their immortality prevents them from facing the moment of truth that death necessitates for the hero. Instead, Benjamin believes, Shakespeare was concerned to show the devastation of history. Overwhelming forces come to bear on the protagonist, and what he realizes is not that he is unique and his suffering different from all others, but rather that history levels all the same, and his particular suffering can serve only to illustrate the general ruin. Rather than look in *Hamlet* for the catharsis of pity and fear Aristotle taught us to expect in tragedy—we see ourselves in the hero and marvel that he has suffered (for us) so nobly—we should appreciate something altogether different. The end of the protagonist is the end of the world, and the void that opens up reveals to us the other world: in religious terms, the afterlife; in philosophical terms, the ageless, changeless pattern of truth.

Thus Benjamin and these other critics agree that the greatest power in *Hamlet* is negation. We shall return to this insight in other contexts and try to situate it historically, psychologically, and philosophically. Now, it is important to return to the consideration of ways in which Shakespeare and his contemporaries tried to explain madness. Then we can pass on to the more modern attempts and finally reconcile the two categories. A third cause of madness in Elizabethan popular belief—well represented in Shakespeare—is demonic possession (MacDonald). This accounts for the darkest side of sixteenth- and seventeenth-century life in Britain, on the Continent, and in the New World: the persecution of women (and occasionally men) for witchcraft. In *Twelfth Night* Feste is sent in the guise of Sir Topas to taunt Malvolio in his confinement, after his pretentious infatuation with Olivia has been taken as evidence of madness.

Out, hyperbolical fiend! How vexest thou this man! Talkest thou nothing but of ladies?
. . . Fie, thou dishonest Satan! I call thee by the most modest terms, for I am one of those gentle ones that will use the Devil himself with courtesy. (IV.ii.29–37)

This, then, is a parody of the ritual of exorcism: the devil, or one of his agents, who has taken possession of the spirit of the victim, and speaks through him, must be driven out. In *The Winter's Tale* Leontes is suddenly convinced that his wife, Hermione, is adulterously involved with his dear friend Polixenes. Rather than build slowly to this climax, Shakespeare depicts its shocking onset as a case of demonic possession:

> . . . Too hot, too hot!
> To mingle friendship far is mingling bloods.
> I have tremor cordis on me. My heart dances
> But not for joy, not joy . . .
>
> Affection, thy intention stabs the center!
> Thou dost make possible things not so held,
> Communicatest with dreams—how can this be?
> With what's unreal thou coactive art,
> And fellow'st nothing. Then 'tis credent
> Thou mayst cojoin with something, and thou dost,
> And that beyond commision, and I find it,
> And that to the infection of my brains
> And hardening of my brows. (I.ii.108–46)

The imagery suggests copulation: something alien has entered his mind and there engendered something out of nothing. The same thing happens in *Othello*, but there the devil's agent is Iago; Othello, finally realizing the extent of his evil, looks for his cloven hoof. Shakespeare suggests something of the same in *Hamlet*: he is so varied in his description of the Ghost—the soul of the dead king come back from purgatory, a devil from hell, a mere apparition—that we make some connection between its visit and Hamlet's madness. In all these cases, Shakespeare takes contemporary belief and shows its effect on the individual character. Othello might call Iago the devil, but this does not prevent him from seeking vengeance first upon the villain and then upon himself.

Returning to Coddon's comparison of Essex with Hamlet, we can perhaps with greater precision analyze the differences between Elizabethan and modern notions of mental functioning and its aberrations. All of their explanations for madness posit an intrusion of some sort. Their religious beliefs allowed them to consider the possibility of actual alien invasion; their psychology caused them to seek specific traumatic experience; their astrology made planetary movement a factor; their medicine led them to blame glandular secretions. All of these are relatively external factors; none suggests a purely internal cause or self-contained collapse. Coddon works analogously, under the influence of the theorist of cultural forces, Michel Foucault. She plays with the term "subjectivity": Essex lacked a proper sense of himself as independent "subject"; he was "subject" to Elizabeth, and any renunciation of her authority meant to his contemporaries madness. One of the great accomplishments of the Renaissance in Western Europe—which, though it came relatively late to England, can be considered relatively complete by 1600—was the integration of a sense of self, separate and apart from social, political, and religious function:

In the Middle Ages . . . man was conscious of himself only as a member of race, people, party, family or corporation—only through some general category. In Italy this veil was first melted into thin air; an objective treatment and consideration of the state and of all things of this world became possible. The subjective side, at the same time, asserted itself with correspopnding emphasis: man became a special individual, and he recognized himself as such. (Burckhardt 100)

Conceptions of individual autonomy and its historical determinants have changed between Burckhardt and Foucault. The so-called New Historicists working under the influence of the latter do not even allow the use of the term "Renaissance," so brilliantly defined by the former. Now we are to speak of "the early modern period." The work of individuation then continues through its vicissitudes into what we used to call the baroque age. Thus there is conflict with Benjamin, who sees Shakespeare's *Hamlet* as a prefiguration of the German baroque "mourning play." Different images emerge from the different traditions of scholarship and criticism. The relation between inside and outside is differently perceived. Coddon, following other adherents of the New Historicist school, posits an emptiness in the individual, a nothingness at the core of one's being: "Because humanist subjectivity has yet to fully emerge in the late sixteenth century, 'in the interior of [Hamlet's] mystery, there is, in short, nothing' " (Coddon 389, with note on Baker 37). Presumably what these critics are waiting for is the individual's recognition that he is himself a mere function of history, that his "humanism" is simply a myth of classical origin; in other words, he lacks the insight into the relation between history and the individual's sense of himself that began with Marx and advanced with Foucault into the current fashion of "historicizing the self."

For Benjamin, the nothing in *Hamlet* is not within but without. It is the relentlessness of court intrigue, the natural treachery of man, which, like the force of fate, finally overcomes the figure who had so consistently railed against it:

Hamlet, as is clear from his conversation with Osric, wants to breathe in this suffocating air of fate in one deep breath. He wants to die by some accident, and as the fateful stage properties gather around him, as [hounds] around their lord and master, the drama of fate flares up in the conclusion of this *Trauerspiel*, as something that is contained, but of course overcome, in it. Whereas tragedy ends with a decision—however uncertain this may be—there resides in the essence of the *Trauerspiel* and especially in the death-scene, an appeal of the kind which martyrs utter. (Benjamin 137)

Benjamin's reference is to that favorite scene of baroque painting: the martyr lies prostrate on the executioner's block—his entrails extracted or his extremities burned off—but he looks in rapture beyond the mortification of his body to the opening in the clouds above, where cherubs beckon his soul to bliss. The nothingness of the world is then all too real in the physical sense, but true reality lies beyond and is defined by the complete negation of everything here and now. It can be argued, of course, that Hamlet knows himself only by negation—that, like Hegel's description of the romantic spirit (*die schöne Seele*), he defines himself only by what he rejects (not seeing himself in the rejected qualities). It comes down to knowledge then. Even if *Hamlet* does not meet the expectations that both Benjamin and the New Historicists have of tragedy, it is difficult to deny to Hamlet his moment of truth, his *anagnorisis*. He consistently refuses to find anything in the world worth committing himself to, but then in choosing action of a futile, fated kind, he does act in the full knowledge that his death is the likely result. We should compare Iphigenia in Euripides' play *Iphigenia in Aulis*. She chooses to sacrifice herself for a false cause—the pan-Hellenic campaign against Troy— but the act of choosing itself is heroic, therefore tragic, and shows a degree of self-consciousness perhaps uncharacteristic of so young and innocent a victim (Aristotle's own criticism of Euripides). On the question of Hamlet's acceptance of fate, we must later consider the argument that here Shakespeare illustrates the late sixteenth-century conflict between Catholic and Protestant views of man's control over his destiny: it has been suggested that bending one's will to accept God's providence is more in line with Protestant belief.

We continue to question what Shakespeare's contemporaries and our own expect of human awareness. We have already seen that Shakespeare, perhaps following Kyd, plays with the word "self" so as to suggest some sense of inward reality. We should remind ourselves that there were no philosophers contemporary with Shakespeare who could produce coherent and consistent systems of thought to define man's place in the universe. As P. Kristeller has said of the Italian humanists, including even Ficino and Bruno, "The Renaissance produced no philosopher of the very first importance" (*Renaissance Philosophy* 1). In the generation after Shakespeare's death, however, three figures—one in England, two on the Continent—did emerge with systematic philosophies: Thomas Hobbes, G. W. Leibniz, and Joachim Spinoza. All thought and wrote in response to René Descartes, whom we might credit with the first attempt to think oneself into being. The famous declaration, *Cogito, ergo sum*, came as Descartes sat alone in a room heated by an earthenware stove: he could doubt the existence of the stove, even of the room, but because he could think of the stove and the room, he *himself* must exist:

Then, examining with attention what I was, and seeing that I could pretend that I had no body and that there was no world nor any place where I was, but that I could not pretend, on that account, that I did not exist; and that, on the contrary, from the very fact that I thought about doubting the truth of other things, it followed very evidently and very certainly that I existed. On the other hand, had I simply stopped thinking, even if all the rest of what I have ever imagined were true, I would have no reason to believe that I existed, from this I knew that I was a substance the whole essence or nature of which was merely to think, and which, in order to exist, needed no place and depended on no material thing. Thus this "I", that is a soul through which I am what I am, is entirely distinct from the body, and is even easier to know than the body, and even if there were no body, the soul would not cease to be all that it is. (*Discourse on Method* IV)

Can we imagine Hamlet making such a statement? Was Shakespeare capable of thinking in this methodical way? All of the great soliloquies are negative in tone and content: against women, against suicide, against his own hesitation, against military action. The most positive speeches are those shared with Horatio:

> Since my dear soul was mistress of her choice
> And could of men distinguish her election,
> Sh'ath sealed thee for herself. For thou hast been
> As one in suffering all that suffers nothing,
> A man that fortune's buffets and rewards
> Hast ta'en with equal thanks. (III.ii.68–73)

Certainly here we have a sense that Hamlet sees in Horatio the opposite of those lizards Rosencrantz and Guildenstern, who change color with their surroundings, and in appreciating his friend's constancy, he also shows some sense of that quality in himself. If he cannot reason his way through to the course of action demanded by the Ghost, then he will not pursue it. He will certainly not do anything for mere convention's sake.

Later in the graveyard, again in conference with Horatio, he considers curiously that Alexander and Caesar were reduced to dust and earth, and in that form suffered reduction to absurd functions: to patch a wall or plug a beer barrel (V.i.225–39). He thus contemplates his own death and, having dismissed all notions of a life hereafter, commits himself to action here and now. Finally, before the duel with Laertes, he again confides with Horatio:

> . . . The interim is mine,
> And a man's life's no more than to say "One." (V.ii.73–74)

. . . we defy augury. There's special providence in the fall of a sparrow. If it be now, 'tis not to come; if it be not to come, it will be now; if it be not now, yet it will come. The readiness is all. Since no man of aught he leaves, knows aught, what is't to leave betimes? (V.ii.215–20)

In facing death, he figures himself; he knows himself first in the contemplation of his negation in death. If we ponder this for a moment—conceiving of the whole play as the protagonist's preparation for death, with dismissals of all the conventional wisdom that makes the prospect of death, and therefore any action that threatens it, appalling—then we might see *Hamlet* as the necessary precursor of Descartes.

Hobbes, too, in his political theory as in his philosophy generally, dismissed conventional wisdom:

The felicity of life consisteth not in the repose of a mind satisfied. For there is no such *finis ultimus*, utmost aim, no *summum bonum*, greatest good, as is spoken of in the books of the old moral philosophers. Nor can a man any more live, whose desires are at an end, than he whose sense and imaginations are at a stand. Felicity is a continual progress of the desire, from one object to another, the attaining of the former being still but the way to the latter. . . . So that in the first place, I put for a general inclination of all mankind, a perpetual and restless desire of power after power, that ceaseth only in death. (*Leviathan* XI)

The "old moral philosophers" are Plato, Aristotle, and Cicero, who became the basis of the three schools of thought that dominated Europe from the late medieval period through the Renaissance: the Platonists, the Scholastics, and the Humanists. Their thinking is metaphysical in that it postulates the absolute existence of such abstract qualities as justice, mercy, truth, and beauty, or in a determined evolution toward perfection. Hobbes is a nominalist and a materialist, believing that abstracts exist only in language; hence there is no form or idea of justice out there against which I can measure my practice of justice here and now. Hobbes's function was like Shakespeare's: to sweep away old beliefs and open up a space for new thinking. Men do not govern in such a way as to approximate the absolute form of justice; that does not exist. Men govern so as to acquire power over other men and prevent other men from acquiring power over them—exactly the opposite of what Plato argued in the *Republic*. Hobbes applied to man's political behavior the principles Galileo had observed in planetary movement: each body is moved by its own forces of attraction and aversion to other bodies. The universal force of gravity had yet to be recognized, and when it was by Newton, a political equivalent was found by John Locke: human understanding. In the meantime, men were thought of as automata, each driven by his own unique and mysterious inner force.

The other two great philosophers of the mid-seventeenth century, Leibniz and Spinoza, think differently. They return to metaphysics but build their systems on scientific observation. Like Descartes, they are immersed in the physical sciences. Both Descartes and Spinoza were specialists in optics—how visual images are transmitted to the human eye and transformed in the human brain. All three attempted to devise unified and universal systems of knowledge. Whereas Descartes left only rudimentary notes in this direction—Leibniz complained that his *Discourse on Method* showed no method—Leibniz and Spinoza arrived at strikingly similar epistemologies and ontologies (studies of "how we know" and "what is," respectively). Leibniz took from Neoplatonism the concept of the monad, that unity that envelops a multiplicity. He insisted, however, on the integrity of the individual soul or element: "all things are contained in all things," so that if a man has perfect knowledge of the present state of an individual thing, he should be able to deduce its whole past and future state, and even the past and future states of the whole universe. Thus, "monads have no windows": they know what is going on outside through the effect of the outside on their own bodies, and such effects mirror their causes. Spinoza has a similar unifying worldview. He contradicts the body-mind dualism of Descartes. There is a hierarchy in nature contained in and culminating in God. His sequence is the same as Aristotle's (inorganic, vegetable, animal, human), but he explains their relations dynamically: the more an individual acts without changing, the more real it is. To express this, he takes a term from Hobbes, *conatus* (traceable back to Aristotle's *dynamis*, or "potential") and makes the motto, *Conatus in suo esse perservandi* ("the inclination of the individual to persist in its own essence"). We immediately see the ethical implications of these two elaborate philosophical systems. They are an attempt to see in patterns of being the definable and predictable regularity of mathematical formulas. They begin then with the physical properties—extension, motion—and build to universal causes. (Hobbes had sought in political behavior the predictability of Galileo's formulations for planetary movement.) God is in the machine. Almost by definition, a metaphysical system will posit some unifying, self-defining force.

I suggest that Shakespearean tragedy is not just an accidental accompaniment to this philosophical development but rather an integral part thereof. Throughout Shakespeare's work, we can find evidence of his impatience with outdated beliefs. In the comedies, he shows us the cost in human suffering of men's outrageous expectations of women. Thus he strikes at the foundations of that most elaborate medieval structure, the courtly love tradition. In the histories, he shows how fragile the old feudal relations between king and subjects can be, how necessary some sort of accommodation whereby the king ingratiates himself and makes himself synonymous with the state. In the tragedies, there is similar examination of traditional ways of looking at individual responsibility and a discarding of the outdated and ineffectual. His heroes do not seek God's approval for their actions, nor do they hold themselves up to absolute standards. Rather they weigh carefully their own needs and desires against the expectations of others. Hamlet refuses to be the revenge hero, although myth and previous drama had taught the audience to expect that of him. This emphasis on the peculiar circumstances of the individual seems almost essential to tragedy. M. Nussbaum has recently argued that Greek tragedy fills a particular ethical need, different from the great metaphysical system of Plato, which followed soon after. Sophoclean heroes do not reason deductively, as Socrates teaches his disciples to do in Plato's dialogues. They do not attempt to define virtues in their ideal state, but rather to work through their own experience to some way of thinking and acting that is peculiarly theirs. In spite of the significant difference between characterization in Greek and Shakespearean tragedy—Greek tragedy is more concerned with the circumstance, so sometimes there is an appearance of inconsistency in the characterization; Shakespearean tragedy puts the character first and then invents circumstance to illustrate him—nevertheless they share an insistence on the here and now. When Hamlet frees himself for action by deciding there is no afterlife to fear, he achieves the same freedom Oedipus has through Sophocles' play, because the Greeks took no interest in an afterlife.

Provisionally, then, we make the proposition that tragedy is antimetaphysical and historically determined. It comes at a time in intellectual history when great systems of belief are breaking up and new ones are yet to be fully formulated. Although tragedy is often cited by philosophers to prove their general principles, tragic poets themselves do not do philosophy. They force their heroes into impossible situations and yet do not equip them with systematic ways of thinking that might refine their responses and alleviate their suffering. Rather, tragedy isolates the individual and makes his suffering unique. This, then, is another reason that *Hamlet* and *Oedipus* are so often cited for excellence in their genre and so often compared.

THEOLOGICAL CONTEXT

The elements of the play that appear to be predominantly, if not peculiarly, Catholic are the Ghost's reference to purgatory (I.v.9–13) and the last rites—"unhousel'd, disappointed, unanel'd, / No reckoning made" specifies the eu-

charist, confession, and extreme unction (77–78); Claudius's attempt to ab-
solve himself through confession (III.iii)—but he does not show true con-
trition or promise atonement; and the Priest's refusal to bury Ophelia in
hallowed ground (V.i.219–31). The common denominators are two: each occasion is concerned with the afterlife, and in each case some office of the
church is required to save the soul of the petitioner.

Catholics pray for souls in purgatory, require the administration of last rites
before death, and make confession, preferably heard regularly by a priest in
church, a prerequisite for salvation. We always think of the immortality of the
soul as the essential belief of all Christianity, and therefore certainly Catholic.
P. Kristeller points out that it did not officially become part of Catholic dogma
until the Lateran Council of 1513 (181–96). The immortality of the soul is
certainly implied in Jesus' teaching in the New Testament. Some of his last
words on the cross were to his fellow sufferers: "We shall be together with my
Father in Heaven." His resurrection then becomes a pattern for all the faithful:
believe in him and know eternal life. But why, then, are the offices of the
church necessary for salvation? Luther argued on the contrary that faith alone
and the Bible (*sola fides et scriptura*) ensured salvation; we are saved not by
either the church or our good deeds but by God's grace alone. If we decide
that the Catholic elements in *Hamlet* are intrusive, that they call attention to
themselves, then how does this affect our reading of its major themes?

It is possible that Catholicism was associated with the revenge tragedy.
Spain and Italy, where these dramas are usually set, are Catholic countries.
Shakespeare might have wanted to invoke that particular conjuction of family
obligation and religious belief. Church and family are both authorities and
usually thought almost synonymous, but in the case of vengeance, they come
into conflict: "Vengeance is mine," sayeth the Lord, and even the Ghost says
of Gertrude, "Leave her to Heaven." Do we consider *Hamlet's* sense of identity differently if we accept him as a Catholic, living in a Catholic country?
Denmark was a Protestant country in Shakespeare's time, with close ties to
Wittenberg, where Luther nailed up his theses and Hamlet is said to have been
educated. We have already noted that some critics see Hamlet's appeal to "a
special providence in the fall of a sparrow" (V.ii.215) as a possible reference
to the prominence of God's providence in Protestant, especially Calvinist, belief. If so, there might be some contrast between the active, aggressive pursuit
of vengeance expected of the Catholic nobleman of the revenge tragedy (even
though it defies his church) and the passive acceptance of the Protestant intellectual (Westine 232–33, in Clayton). There is also possibly a contrast between the medieval ideals of chivalry appropriate to the historical setting of
Hamlet and Shakespeare's representation of its action as taking place in a Re-

naissance court. (Of course, the world of Hamlet depicted by Saxo is prechivalric and pre-Christian, for which Belleforest apologized to his gentler readers.)

I would like to pursue briefly the parodox of the militant Catholic. If Shakespeare had wanted to invoke as antitype to his characterization of Hamlet the figure of the young aristocrat, devout in his faith and willing to die for it, he had ready at hand, in his own family, the mission and martyrdom of the young poet and Jesuit Robert Southwell. Shakespeare was born (1563) just after the rule of the Catholic Queen Mary (1553–1558), who was called "Bloody" for her persecution of Protestants; most of his life was spent under the rule of Queen Elizabeth (1558–1603). Since she was the head of the Church of England (Defender of the Faith), to worship as a Catholic was an act of treason.

In Shakespeare's own family in Warwickshire there were many Catholics. Southwell, a distant cousin on his mother's side, was not only a practicing Catholic but a Jesuit, a member of that order founded by St. Ignatius of Loyola to spread the faith among unbelievers. In England that meant celebrating mass in secret for familes who kept the faith. In 1592 Southwell was apprehended for that offense and tortured so that he would confess his crimes and implicate others. Ten times he was strung up by his hands, so as to suffer all the agonies of the crucifixion, but cut down just before the strain on his muscles would have ruptured his organs and brought on death. Then he languished in filth and deprivation in the Tower of London for three years and was finally brought to the block for execution. This would have meant being hung by the neck but cut down while still conscious, then to have watched as his entrails were extracted and burned before him, and finally to have his limbs torn from his body ("hanged, drawn, and quartered"). Some benevolent bystander with the power to abbreviate the proceedings allowed Southwell to expire by the rope (Devlin 274–90).

Southwell left behind a literature of meditation, including "Saint Peter's Complaint," "Mary Magdalen's Tears," and "Triumph over Death" (Milward 54–58). The dedication for the first of these is "To my worthy good cousin, Master W.S." In prose he complains: "Poets, by abusing their talents and making the follies and feignings of love the customary subject of their base endeavors, have so discredited this faculty that a poet, a lover and a liar are by many reckoned but three words of one signification." The dedication continues in verse:

> This makes my mourning muse dissolve in tears;
> This themes my heavy pen—too plain in prose;
> Christ's thorn is sharp, no head his garland wears;
> Still finest wits are stilling Venus' rose;

> In paynim toys the sweetest veins are spent;
> To Christian works few have their talents lent.

It is easy to hear in the prose portion an echo of Theseus's speech in *A Mid-summer Night's Dream*, "the lunatic, the lover and the poet" (V.i.7) and in the verse a reference to Shakespeare's "Venus and Adonis." We might presume that Southwell in captivity saw his cousin's work in manuscript and chided him for wasting his God-given powers on such trivial matters as erotic attachments. He then makes the clear contrast between pleasures of the flesh and mortification of the flesh (Christ's torture and crucifixion), concentration on this life, and meditation on the next.

When Shakespeare came to write *Hamlet*—we have no way of knowing when he began this project, but it was no later than 1599, four years after Southwell's death and the posthumous publication of his work—he seems to have echoed passages from "Triumph over Death." Southwell writes to comfort the countess of Arundel for the death of a female relative: "If this departure [i.e., death] be grievous, it is also common." Gertrude speaks of his father's death to Hamlet: "Thou know'st 'tis common." Southwell says, "Some live till they be weary of life," and Hamlet admits to Rosencrantz and Guildenstern, "I have of late, but wherefore I know not, lost all my mirth, foregone all custom of exercise." Southwell tells us that "as prisoners we are kept in ward," and Hamlet sees the world as a prison "in which there are many confines, wards and dungeons." The blurring of the boundary between sleep and death is a common theme to both:

> You still float in a troublesome sea . . .
> As one rather falling asleep than dying, she most
> happily took her leave of all mortal miseries . . .
> The general tide wafteth all passengers to the same shore.

> . . . To die—to sleep,
> No more; and by a sleep to say we end
> The heartache and the thousand natural shocks
> That flesh is heir to . . .
> . . . Who would fardels bear,
> To grunt and sweat under a weary life,
> But that the dread of something after death,
> The undiscover'd country, from whose bourn
> No traveler returns, puzzles the will. (III.i.64–80)

Finally Southwell holds out the prospect

that fear of a speedy passage might keep us in readiness and hope of a longer continuance cut off unripe cares.

Hamlet finally insists to Horatio, "The readiness is all," just as Edgar consoles Gloucester:

> . . . Men must endure
> Their going hence even as their coming hither.
> Ripeness is all. (*Lear* V.ii.9–11)

(I owe the comparison of these passages to Milward.)

We might say then that Southwell gives us new understanding of *Hamlet*. Southwell makes love to death, while he accuses Shakespeare in his earlier career of worshiping love. Though we cannot claim that Southwell's appeal to Shakespeare inspired him to turn from the primarily erotic interests of the early poems and comedies, nevertheless the verbal and thematic parallels do urge us to see something of Southwell in Hamlet. Certainly in Southwell we see a Catholic stoicism in the face of death that might just as easily lie behind the resolution with which Hamlet finally faces death, as the Protestant yielding to the providence of God. Southwell also enriches our notion of melancholy.

We have noted that the Elizabethan convention was twofold: disparagement of the ways of the world (especially the court) and lovesickness. Southwell expresses a *taedium vitae*, or world weariness, that is much more profound, and again it is eroticized. He looks beyond the trivial cares of this world to a kind of ecstatic contentment in the next. We can understand his immediate motives for writing such meditations; he was literally on the rack. Whereas Southwell suffered physical torment and saw no escape from it but death—to which he then reconciled himself—Hamlet's torment is mental and emotional. T. S. Eliot found dissatisfaction in *Hamlet* as a work of art because Hamlet's suffering is "in excess of its actual causes." Perhaps if we look beyond Southwell to Loyola himself, we might find some further significance in Shakespeare's evocation of the militant Catholic mystic in this play.

Ignatius of Loyola (1491–1556) was born into a noble family in the north of Spain and entered military service. He was crippled by a cannonball in 1522, and as he lay near death in his family's castle underwent a religious conversion. Upon his recovery, he traveled to Paris to study theology. He then began work on a systematic guide to meditation, which he called *Spiritual Exercises*. He organized the Society of Jesus under the patronage of Pope Paul III in 1540. These Jesuits then became the defenders of papal supremacy in the battle against the Protestant reformation, combining two types of discipline: their spiritual exercises taught them the absolute authority of God and the necessity of subjecting their will to his; they saw themselves as the army of the pope and thus followed him unquestioning, with military fervor. Although the issues are combined so as to inhibit easy associations, it seems that Shakespeare presents in the character of Hamlet himself—and in the contrast between Hamlet and Fortinbras—some aspects of the conflict between Protestant reformers, represented by his schooling in Wittenberg, where his classmate was Horatio, whose philosophy is skeptical (I.v.174–75), and Catholic retrenchment, represented by certain resemblances to Loyola.

In an elaborate metaphor, Hamlet compares his mind to a copybook. The Ghost demands, "Remember me," and Hamlet responds:

> . . . Remember thee?
> Yea, from the table of my memory
> I'll wipe away all trivial fond records,
> All saws of books, all forms, all pressures past
> That youth and observation copied there,
> And thy commandment all alone shall live
> Within the book and volume of my brain,
> Unmix'd with baser matter. Yes, by heaven!
> O most pernicious woman!
> O villain, villain, smiling damned villain!
> My tables. Meet it is I set it down
> That one may smile, and smile, and be a villain—
> At least I am sure it may be so in Denmark. (I.v.97–109)

Hamlet later enters at Act II, scene ii, line 68, "reading on a book." The matter of that book later appears to be satirical. Contemporary advice to the courtier is that he should carry a copybook always with him, as a means to record clever turns of phrase. Jenkins cites at Act I, scene v, line 107 a contemporary warning to test "the correspondence of a man's words and deeds by noting them on 'a table.'" Hypocrisy is the point, then, and the book is the record by which one can catch the hypocrite in contradiction.

J. de Gilbert quotes from the autobiography of Loyola and other sources on his habits:

His intention was to pass only a few days there in a hospital and "to enter some notes into his copybook which he carefully carried with him, and which gave him much consolation." This was the copybook into which he had already begun at Loyola to transcribe the more notable words and deeds of the life of Christ and the saints. This care to note down the thoughts and observations which might help others was another of his lifelong traits. (27)

In the order of the *Spiritual Exercises*, we see the contrast between the falseness of the temporal world and the truth of the divine. One begins with an examination of one's conscience and a meditation on sin and hell (first week), then moves on to contemplation of the Incarnation and Nativity (second week), then to the Passion (third week) and finally to the love of God (fourth week). Loyola could experience a mystical intimacy with God:

Sometimes when my understanding rose up above without any willing of my own, I thought I could behold something of the divine Being which otherwise, even had I so willed, I never felt it in my power to behold. (Rahner 4)

We recall that Southwell's meditations include "Saint Peter's Complaint" and "Mary Magdalen's Tears." From Loyola's autobiographical notes we learn that tears can be a physical sign of a spiritual union with God:

The gift of tears should not be asked for in any absolute way. It is not necessary, and it is not good or profitable either absolutely or for all persons. . . . Some have the gift because their nature is such that in them the affections in the higher part of the soul have their reaction in the lower part, or because God sees that the gift would be profitable for them and grants it. (de Gilbert 64)

He also recommends mortification of the flesh, in moderation:

The third kind of penance is to chastise the body, that is, to inflict sensible pain upon it. This is done by wearing hairshirts, cords, or iron chains on the body, or by scourging or wounding oneself, and by other kinds of austerities. (*Spiritual Exercises* 85.3)

The more suitable and safe form of penance seems to be that which would cause sensible pain to the body and not penetrate to the bones, so that it inflicts pain, but does not cause sickness. For this reason it would seem suitable to chastise oneself with light cords that cause superficial pain, rather than in any other way that might bring about a serious internal infirmity. (*Spiritual Exercises* 86)

One does to oneself what the torturers did to Southwell, all in the effort to separate body and soul, to remind oneself that the body is only here and now, but the soul is eternal and will be united with God after death.

Loyola's precepts found expression in an English devotional published in 1582, *The Christian Dictionary*, by the Jesuit Robert Persons. As with Southwell's meditations, Persons's entries have resonance with Hamlet's speeches (Milward 45):

. . . that body, which was before so delicately entertained, whereupon the wind might not be suffered to blow, nor the sun to shine . . . is left for a prey to be devoured of worms.

Hamlet considers in his first soliloquy his father's attitude toward his mother:

> . . . so loving to my mother
> That he might not beteem the winds of heaven
> Visit her face too roughly. (I.ii.140–42)

Persons considers the contradictions in the human condition; the earth is . . .

enriched with estimable and endless treasure, and yet itself standing, or rather hanging, with all the weight and poise, in the midst of the air, as a little ball without prop or pillar. (Milward 46)

Hamlet contemplates the universe:

this goodly frame the earth seems to me a sterile promontory, this most excellent canopy the air, look you, this brave o'erhanging firmament, this majestical roof fretted with golden fire, why, it appeareth nothing to me but a foul and pestilent congregation of vapours. (II.ii.298–303)

Sometimes the passages are so close that it seems Shakespeare is making a parody of the original, or rather that these sorts of meditation were so common in his time that he could put them in the mouth of Hamlet and simultaneously impress his audience with Hamlet's source of despair and gently ridicule its excess. Man must suffer:

he shall see justice sold, verity wrested, shame lost, and equity disguised. He shall see the innocent condemned, the guilty delivered, the wicked advanced, the virtuous depressed. (Milward 46)

Hamlet thinks of the abuses that make suicide attractive:

> For who would bear the whips and scorns of time,
> Th'oppressor's wrong, the proud man's contumely,
> The pangs of dispriz'd love, the law's delay,
> The insolence of office, and the spurns
> That patient merit of th'unworthy takes,
> When he himself might his quietus make
> With a bare bodkin? (III.i.70–76)

Finally Persons warns us that we shall be naked of all wordly comforts when we meet our end:

where will all your delights, recreations and vanities be? all your pleasant pastimes? all your pride and bravery in apparel? your glistening in gold? your wanton dalliance pleasant entertainments? (Milward 46)

Hamlet in the graveyard asks the skull of Yorick:

Where be your gibes now, your gambols, your songs, your flashes of merriment. . . .
Now get you to my lady's chamber and tell her, let her paint an inch thick, to this
favour she must come. (V.i.183–88)

This obsession with death is downright medieval. In the twelfth, thirteenth,
and fourteenth centuries, the wealthiest and most accomplished nobles retired
to monasteries in their middle age to await and prepare for death. Loyola and
his followers reintroduce this kind of meditation into early modern life. In
Hamlet, then, we find a Jesuit's consciousness of death—and its contrast with
and contradiction of life—joined with a young Renaissance intellectual's
skepticism about spiritual concerns and delight in such amusements as the
theatre. (Of course, it was the Protestants who were always trying to close the
theatres.)

Some large issues that the question of religion raises are the source of
Hamlet's sense that nothing is worth doing here and now because all the
things of this world are nought; the extent and significance of Hamlet's identification with the suffering of Christ; the motivation behind changes in his attitude after the sea voyage. Ultimately we shall have to ask what difference it
makes that Hamlet finally stops worrying about damnation in a life to come
and exerts himself here and now. Does this represent a religious conversion or,
rather, a conversion from religion to philosophy?

PHILOSOPHICAL CONTEXT

There are essentially two different meanings of "philosophy," the one popular or "vulgar," the other technical. Montaigne uses the first when he says, "To
philosophize is to learn to die." We speak of someone being philosophical if
he seeks solace from proverbial wisdom or puts his own immediate misfortune in some kind of long-range perspective. There is much of this in *Hamlet*.
In the second scene, for instance, Claudius and Gertrude both tell Hamlet that
he should not take the loss of his father as a tragedy "particular" to him, since
the loss of fathers is "common." An extension of this kind of philosophy is
what constitutes the soliloquies. Hamlet keeps asking himself why he cannot
seek vengeance for his father, why his mother is sexually incontinent, how the
world has gone wrong. It is this aspect of Hamlet that caused the Romantic
critics to distinguish him as an intellectual, one who for "consider[ing] too curiously" on the significance of events fails to take part in them. We can say
then that Hamlet is philosophical by nature, that it is part of his character to
question and compare, to seek the relation between his own circumstances and
those generally prevailing in the world. This can lead us to a determination of

the difference between Hamlet's psychology—his misogyny, for instance—and his philosophy—his insistence that a course of action, like revenge, must be rationally chosen rather than imposed. The two are intimately related, of course, but to say this particular thing is not easy for me to do is not the same as saying nothing in this world is worth doing.

The second, more precise definition of philosophy is a system of thought that is internally coherent, whether or not it completely congrues with experience of the world. Thus Plato's Theory of the Forms is more precisely philosophical for the very reason that it contradicts our sense impressions of the world. He tells us that what we experience here and now is only a vague, distorted reflection of the true Forms of things, which have a separate and independent existence elsewhere. Our investigation here will be into Hamlet's curious considerations, whether they are systematically coherent, and whether they resemble any philosophy we associate with thinkers prior to Shakespeare, contemporary with him, or even those who have followed. In this last case we shall follow the precept of H. Fraenkel: "I do not adhere to the doctrine that we have no right to ascribe to a thinker a notion for the unequivocal expression of which he possessed and used no specific tool. Quite to the contrary: It is perfectly normal for this or that concept to have existed in a person's mind in a less definitive form, long before someone else couched it in dry and set philosophical phraseology" (xi).

In other plays, we find Shakespeare considering positions that are technically philosophical. In *Romeo and Juliet* and *1 Henry IV*, he considers nominalism, the position that abstract qualities exist only in language. Thus Juliet asks:

> Romeo, Romeo, wherefore art thou Romeo?
> Deny thy father and refuse thy name.
> Or if thou wilt not, be but sworn my love
> And I'll no longer be a Capulet. . . .
> 'Tis but thy name that is my enemy:
> Thou art thyself, though not a Montague.
> What's Montague? It is not hand nor foot
> Nor arm nor face nor any other part
> Belonging to a man. O be some other name.
> What's in a name? That which we call a rose
> By any other name would smell as sweet. (II.ii.33–44)

Falstaff wonders:

What is in that word honor? What is that honor? Air. A trim reckoning! Who hath it? He that died o' Wednesday. Doth he feel it? No. Doth he hear it? No. 'Tis insensible then? Yea, to the dead. But will it not live with the living? No. Why? Detraction will not suffer it. Therefore I'll none of it. Honor is a mere scutcheon. And so ends my catechism. (V.i.135–43)

We are not to think that Shakespeare halts the action of his play to allow his characters speculation on philosophical questions current in his day, nor are we to take these passages as mere parody of philosophical speculation, which we certainly do find elsewhere, as in the graveyard scene of *Hamlet*, for instance. Rather, Shakespeare in these passages transfers philosophical speculation into dramatic situations where its immediate importance to particular persons can be appreciated. "Philosophy in action," or "applied philosophy," or "practical philosophy"—none of these quite catches what Shakespeare accomplishes. He takes philosophy out of the study and puts it to work in situations where characters have to make choices. Can Juliet love a member of the family her family hates? Will Falstaff fight? Shakespeare chooses to frame his characters' responses to their own particular problems within a tradition of thinking about the relation between words and things. Since the twelfth century, nominalism had been a way theologians thought and wrote about Christian virtues; if they were not careful, they could fall into the heresy of thinking about God himself that way. Since Juliet later tells Romeo to swear by himself, she puts him in the place of God. In a very complicated way, then, Shakespeare has Juliet express herself precisely so that she literally puts Romeo at the center of her universe and cancels out all her other relations. Her family becomes just a name; his family becomes just a name; names are not things; the existence of the individual is not threatened by his contradiction of such social conventions as naming. Therefore, one way of seeing their tragedy is as their failure to remake the world into their own image, where their love defines their relationship, not names.

Falstaff will not die for honor. He proves it is only a word, a mere escutcheon—that insignia that warriors painted on their shields. Throughout the play, Shakespeare contrasts Hotspur, for whom such feudal ideals as honor actually exist—he claims he can catch her by the hair and save her from drowning (I.iii.201–8)—and Falstaff, whose existence is only corporeal, unleavened by aspiration for anything beyond himself. Here that contrast culminates in this reference to the technique of theological disputation (catechism). Falstaff proves that honor is only a word, that like other abstract qualities it has its existence only in language.

Where in *Hamlet* do we find such references to the technical workings of philosophy? Perhaps in the first exchange with Rosencrantz and Guildenstern:

Hamlet: What have you, my good friends, deserv'd at the hands of Fortune, that she sends you to prison hither?

Guildenstern:	Prison, my lord?
Hamlet:	Denmark's a prison.
Rosencrantz:	Then is the world one.
Hamlet:	A goodly one, in which there are many confines, wards, and dungeons, Denmark being one o' the worst.
Rosencrantz:	We think not so, my lord.
Hamlet:	Why, then 'tis none to you'; for there is nothing either good or bad but thinking makes it so. To me it is a prison.
Rosencrantz:	Why then your ambition makes it one. 'Tis too narrow for your mind. (II.ii.242–53)

This sequence resembles the opening of *The Merchant of Venice*, where Salanio and Salerio question Antonio about his melancholy, trying to convince him that he is overly concerned about his business ventures abroad, when, in fact, we soon find out that it is his erotic attachment to Bassanio that depresses him; it is libidinal rather than financial investment that has made him feel depleted.

A similar turn takes place here in *Hamlet*, since the sequence ends—after Hamlet's long speech beginning, "I have of late . . . lost all my mirth"—with Rosencrantz's silent quibble on "Man delights not me." But Hamlet's line, "For there is nothing either good or bad, but thinking makes it so," suggests the philosophical position of relativism, or perceptivism. We associate this position originally with the fifth-century Greek Sophist Protagoras, who maintained, "Man is the measure of all things, things that are that they are, and things that are not that they are not." More generally, this philosophical position might be associated with skepticism—the belief that people cannot certainly know the things of this world, and that even if one person thinks he or she does know, this person's thinking will be different from and incommunicable to another. This position we associate with another Sophist, Gorgias. Our interest in these figures will become clear when I relate Shakespeare and his philosophical questioning to Greek tragedy and its philosophical background. We shall find that in both cases, the drama actualizes and personalizes the general principles worked out in the more theoretical discipline.

If we analyze Hamlet's statement carefully, we find that it resonates with ambiguity typical of both Shakespeare and philosophical speculation. The first and most important double meaning we notice is that of the verb "is": does it represent the simple copulative or the existential sense of "to be," that is, "Nothing is either good or bad, but thinking makes it so," or "Nothing exists—whether good or bad—but thinking that it exists makes it exist (for the person thinking)"? This latter reading brings Hamlet very close indeed to Protagoras's radical position. If we accept this reading here, then we shall have to reread the "To be, or not to be" soliloquy differently later. There we shall have to consider whether, in addition to the contemplation of suicide, there is also the contemplation on the nature of being; "the question" might be whether what happens "in the mind" is what makes the difference between being and nonbeing, or not being. In both passages, there is the conjunction of the antithesis of being and nonbeing with the power of the mind, with thinking. We associate Hamlet with thinking and see in the play that this quality sets him off from the rest of the characters, who seem to drive on to their goals without too much troubling their minds. If we determine that Hamlet's thinking is so radical as to question the actual existence of things in the world—only thinking makes them so—then we must link this with his thinking that he is unique, that only he "is" rather than seeming to be (I.ii.75), and that no person can know the world of another's thinking: "to know a man well were to know himself" (V.i.133).

We need not hark back to the ancient Greek philosophers to find this kind of meditation. Skepticism is Montaigne's philosophical position, at least throughout the first two books of *Essais*. These were not available in English until John Florio's translation was published in 1603, and it is difficult to prove that Shakespeare knew Montaigne firsthand before *The Tempest* in 1611, where he carefully answers Montaigne's argument against ethnocentrism as developed in the essay "On Cannibals." Nevertheless, he could have had access to either an original French edition, available from 1580, or Florio's translation might have been circulating in manuscript during 1599–1601. At any rate, Shakespeare meditates in *Hamlet* on the same aspects of man's place in the world as Montaigne does in his "Apology for Raymond Sebond." Consider the sequence of thought in this passage, where Montaigne asks rhetorically where man's confidence in his own reason comes from, and compare it with Hamlet's speech to Rosencrantz and Guildenstern, "I have of late—but wherefore I know not—lost all my mirth" (II.ii.290–304):

Who has persuaded him that that admirable motion of the celestial vault, the eternal light of those torches rolling so proudly above his head, the fearful movements of that infinite sea, were established and have lasted so many centuries for his service? Is it possible to imagine anything so ridiculous as that this miserable and puny creature, who is not even master of himself, exposed to the attacks of all things, should call himself master and emperor of the universe, the least part of which it is not in his power to know, much less to command? (328–29)

Other features of this long essay that also find echoes in *Hamlet* are the consideration of devoted followers' committing suicide after the death of their leader and men following their leaders unquestioningly into battle (337), the relation between melancholy or madness and wisdom (363), the consideration whether Caesar retains his qualities after death (385), speaking of the soul as "she" and friendship as the blending of souls (426), and a pervasive misogyny (401).

Even if we cannot convince ourselves that Shakespeare knew this particular essay of Montaigne before he wrote *Hamlet*—Montaigne's constant reference to and quotation from ancient philosophers adds further force to the argument in favor—we should appreciate that his philosophical positions are congruent with those of Shakespeare. Both represent a questioning of the High Renaissance celebration of man as in control of his mind and his universe. Montaigne makes specific reference to Copernicus's decentering of the earth in the universe, and this, of course, suggests human decentering, since the old worldview saw the universe as God's creation for human benefit. What happens to people's thinking about themselves when they can no longer hold on to the old beliefs: in their likeness to each other, in their prescribed place in the order of things, in their ability to use their reason to impose their own order and control, in their godlike nature? The answer lies in Hamlet's concern with nothing, or nonbeing.

This he articulates in relation to several different but related realms. There is, primarily, his contemplation of suicide, his own nonbeing. It is important to recognize here that his consideration is more complex than the simple equation that death is the cancellation or negation of life. Rather, he considers that death might bring with it worse than nothing—the eternal torment threatened by Christian belief:

> For in that dream of death what dreams may come,
> When we have shuffled off this mortal coil, . . .
> But that the dread of something after death,
> The undiscover'd country, from whose bourn
> No traveller returns, puzzles the will,
> And makes us rather bear those ills we have
> Than fly to others that we know not of? (III.i.66–82)

His father's ghost, though he insists he comes from purgatory, not hell, mentions "secrets of [his] prison-house" which would harrow Hamlet's soul, and produce physical results such as making his hair stand up like a porcupine's (I.v.13–20). Hell, then, is something more than just the absence of life: it represents a contradiction of life in which the sins committed here and now are infinitely repeated, but the desires that led to those sins are never satisfied. Indeed hell is very much like Gertrude's sexual appetite: it seems to grow by what it feeds on.

Another view of death is as a cancellation of the physical:

> O that this too too sullied flesh would melt,
> Thaw and resolve itself into a dew,
> Or that the Everlasting had not fix'd
> His canon 'gainst self-slaughter. (I.ii.129–32)

Here he seems to identify the flesh with his mother and the spirit with his father (Hyperion), so that the longing for death represents the desire to leave the
world of the flesh ("unweeded garden . . . rank and gross") and assimilate with
the spirit world. We might go so far as to claim that Hamlet thinks of death in
terms of an escape from his mother's sexuality. She represents for him a threat
to his identity that he felt protected from as long as his father lived, but now
she is ungovernable, all-consuming. Again, it is a question of negation. We
should consider how the male child comes to conceive some sense of his own
authority in the world through the threat posed to him by the oedipal father.
Only in his fantasy of castration does he see himself as whole. In *Hamlet* there
are both oedipal and anti-oedipal forces operating, so that Hamlet's desire is
for a father who can contain and control the mother. The philosophical proposition that results is that Hamlet defines life through negation. He desires a
cessation of the anxiety that his mother's unchecked sexuality induces in him.
This is like the Christian desire for paradise as a cessation of all the evil that
is let loose in this world. He can define that pure good only as a negation of
this evil, which he knows here and now.

This association of the woman with the negative is brought out in three
scenes: the nunnery scene (III.i), the play within the play scene (III.ii), and the
closet scene (III.iv). In the first, it is clear that the hatred Hamlet feels for his
mother has been extended to Ophelia. Since he is convinced that his mother is
a whore, all women are whores, so he tells Ophelia, "Get thee to a nunnery."
The nunnery is a place of renunciation. The woman there denies or negates her
procreative function, thinking that in this state of purity, focusing all her energy
on contemplation of the life to come and prayers for the salvation of others, she
can cancel out the evil of the world and by her assimilation to Mary contradict
the sin of Eve. (I shall note below that all the garden imagery in the play suggests a lost Eden.) Here, too, though, negation is not simple. Because of Protestant ignorance and prejudice, the monastic life of Catholics is inverted, so that
in popular usage the word "nunnery" is used of the whorehouse. Hamlet thus
sends Ophelia where he thinks she belongs, where perhaps her lust—insatiable
like his mother's—might finally meet its own challenge.

In the play-within-the-play scene, Hamlet plays a word game at Ophelia's
expense:

Hamlet: Lady, shall I lie in your lap?

Ophelia: No, my lord.

Hamlet: I mean my head upon your lap.

Ophelia: Ay, my lord.

Hamlet: Do you think I meant country matters?

Ophelia: I think nothing, my lord.

Hamlet: That's a fair thought to lie between maids' legs.

Ophelia: What is, my lord?

Hamlet: Nothing. (III.ii.110–120)

We are not surprised by Shakespeare's punning or by Hamlet's virulent misogyny, but we must not ignore the philosophical implications of the exchange. First, Hamlet puns on "lie" and "lap," and when Ophelia protests, he blames her, with another pun: "country"/cunt. Her turn of phrase is ambiguous enough to start him going again: "I think nothing" can mean either, "I am not thinking about anything," or, "I am thinking about nothing." How can one think about what does not exist? Hamlet has twice done so, as we have seen. Does thinking about it make it exist? Notoriously, in Shakespeare's bawdy and Freudian theory, a woman's thing is no thing; her vagina is not a penis. Freud theorizes about *Penisnied*, which is usually translated as "penis envy" but is more acurately etymologized as "lack of a penis." When Hamlet replies, "That's a fair thought to lie between maids' legs," his phrase is ambiguous: is it a fair thought for a man to lie between maids' legs, or is there a fair thought lying between maids' legs? Ophelia, as the ingenue, hears the latter, and asks, "What is?" to which Hamlet replies, "Nothing." This is the end of the exchange, and the goal toward which Hamlet always seems to be running. What if the object of desire is nothing, or worse than nothing? Nothing is a lack or an absence, but what if that object is itself a desiring subject, so that the nothing becomes a void that must be filled by the subject in the object, that is, what if the subject becomes the object of the object? This is that other kind of negation: not just the absence of an original presence (e.g., penis) but rather the presence of a negating force that threatens and cancels the original presence (e.g., vagina).

Elsewhere, especially in the *Sonnets*, Shakespeare plays on the Elizabethan convention of calling the vagina "hell." "Hell" is a gaping void that does not simply cancel out life but inverts it: desire there is insatiable. In *Hamlet* Shakespeare puts hell on earth by making Hamlet feel impotent in the face of his mother's desire and then showing his extension of that response to Ophelia. But he is still philosophizing: he thinks of death and he thinks of the woman, and both are more than simple negations of his own being; they are an inversion of it, so that he becomes caught in their desire. Perhaps it is the male equivalent of "the fate worse than death." Hamlet wishes for death as a cessation of desire, but now he faces death as infinite desire. He becomes not Sisyphus constantly rolling the rock up the hill only to have it roll back down again; now he sees himself as the rock. He wants nothing, in both the sense that there is nothing he wants and that he wants the lack of wanting. What he is faced with is much worse. Hamlet needs to put himself up against something that will define him here and now and in the afterlife. Or perhaps he needs to define this life against the afterlife. That nothing would then reveal his about-to-be-lost positive. If I do not know my life here and now, then by contemplating death I might seize on the reversal of that contemplation as this life. For Hamlet this is impossible because the world of negation that he lives in does not offer simply this as a negation of that, but rather this as a complete subversion of that. He grasps at mirror images of himself in Horatio, and even Fortinbras and Laertes, whom he considers unenlightened. But nothing in his experience equips him for the contemplation of the radically obliterating other. To return to the Copernican figure, he becomes like the earth itself caught in the pull of the sun, endlessly circling but without control of his own orbit. And the sun is not the god, his father, but the desire of his mother. To be human then is to be pulled about in a vast force field without poles of demarcation or even clearly anithetical magnetic forces.

Three philosophical systems in particular make use of negation: those of Plato, Hegel, and Heidegger. In each we are asked to define truth, or the world of pure being, by canceling out our immediate experience. These are all systems that propose the existence of a realm of reality beyond the here and now and are thus in this sense metaphysical ("beyond or after the world of nature"). It will be instructive to examine these briefly in order to appreciate Hamlet's position within the tradition of Western intellectual history and within his own play.

Shakespeare is rightly credited with being the first dramatist to develop character in the sense that his characters change over the course of their dramas. Hamlet is the first and best example of this; there is a certain consistency in his speeches over the early acts, but when he returns from England, having had a near-death experience, all this changes. The earlier position might be said to have its summary and final statement in the oft-deleted soliloquy of Act IV: "How all occasions do inform against me!" (IV.iv.32–66). Here, as in the earlier "O what a rogue and peasant slave am I!" (II.ii.530–85), the logic of the speech is comparative. He compares himself with Fortinbras:

> Witness this army of such mass and charge,
> Led by a delicate and tender prince,

> Whose spirit, with divine ambition puff'd,
> Makes mouths at the invisible event,
> Exposing what is mortal and unsure
> To all that fortune, death and danger dare,
> Even for an eggshell. (47–53)

The point here is that action must be taken, but the making of the point involves the juxtaposition of the human element with what cancels that out: death. On the humanistic level, we can say that we do not know ourselves until we are tested, that the event proves the man. Philosophically stated, we come closer to the purer logic of language itself: only in the negation of the given do we comprehend the nature of both the given and the sought-after quotient or definition. We call man mortal because he faces death; death defines the nature of his existence. As a finite being, his essence is expressed in action, and the action in which he risks or approaches death is most definitive.

In Plato's metaphysical system, as developed in the middle dialogues such as *Symposium*, *Phaidros*, and *Republic*, man lives in a world of shifting and uncertain illusions, but can seek through philosophy to comprehend the removed world of Truth and Beauty, a realm of absolute and immutable values. All of Plato's imagery, such as the myth of the cave in the *Republic*, emphasizes the distorting and misleading nature of sense experience. When he suggests the realm of the Forms, he uses imagery suggesting ecstatic or mystical experience: the soul has wings and flies to meet the Forms, or under the influence of erotic attraction one rises higher and higher, escaping the merely physical, and approaching the purely spiritual, which is associated with the thing as it is rather than as it appears to be.

Several of Shakespeare's plays have been analyzed as meditations on Platonic themes, most notably *Two Gentlemen of Verona* and *A Midsummer Night's Dream* (Vyvyan). What is always at issue is the attempt to find in human affairs, especially the erotic, the constancy and immutability of the Forms. The young male lovers of Shakespeare's comedies consistently misjudge the young women they love as fickle and prone to betrayal, the same accusations made in the tragedies against Desdemona and Ophelia. Shakespeare then complicates the basic Platonic contrast between the changeable things of this world and the constancy of the world of the Forms by insisting on perspective. Often we see the constant as inconstant, and vice versa (MacCary, 55–70). He shares this interest in perspective with his contemporaries Descartes among philosophers, Cervantes among litterateurs, and Velázquez and Vermeer among painters. Nothing is, in and of itself, but only as it is seen by a particular subject. More radically, there is a denial of, or at least a lack of interest in, constancy itself, as if these thinkers were admitting, with Protagoras, that each man is the measure of all things (of what is and what is not), and with Pope that the proper study of mankind is man. We therefore err when we read into or out of our actual experience those abstract qualities confined to the other world where age, change, and desire do not intrude.

In Plato there are two important types of dynamic relations that make definition possible. First, there is the dialectic itself, the exchange between two interlocutors that should move toward the definition of the topic under discussion (e.g., What is piety?). In this process various examples of the quality are considered, and some aspects are brought forward in the discussion while others are cast out as irrelevant or contradictory; for example, it is originally suggested that justice consists of doing good for one's friends and harm to one's enemies, but then it is agreed that doing harm to one's enemies is not part of justice. In Hamlet we see this sort of operation in the first exchange with Rosencrantz and Guildenstern; they try to determine what is wrong with Hamlet and attempt to attribute his malaise to ambition, but he resists this. Finally they give up their attempt and simply announce to him the arrival of the players. Even in Plato some of the dialogues are aporetic; it is finally agreed that the process of dialectic has failed to define the topic, and a new attempt must be made.

The other important relationship in Plato is the erotic. The pursuit of philosophy is likened to the erotic exchange between an older man and a younger man. The older man (*erastēs*) sees in the younger man (*erōmenos*) the younger, more beautiful image of himself, and he falls in love with that. The younger man falls in love with the image the older man has of him. As they continue in their commerce together, they gradually refine away all purely physical and individual aspects of their relationship and thus define the essential quality of love. We see the operation of this kind of dialectic most clearly in the *Sonnets*, but also in *Hamlet*, in his relations with Horatio.

In the early nineteenth century German philosopher Georg Wilhem Friedrich Hegel, we find a slightly different form of dialectic and also a variation on the *erastēs-erōmenos* relationship. In his *Phänomenologie des Geistes* Hegel traces the gradual revelation of what he calls Absolute Spirit, which we might compare with Plato's Forms of Truth and Beauty. In Hegel dialectic is characterized by the process of *Aufhebung*, which is both a cancellation and a sublimation. As in Plato, the process is logical, but in Hegel nothing is cast out; everything is carried forward, but raised to a higher degree where seeming contradiction is reconciled. Hegel invokes the example of Sophocles' *Antigone* when he attempts to define justice. He sees in the play a confrontation between the demands of the state, represented by Creon, and the demands of the individual, represented by Antigone, but he insists that the individual must finally recognize herself as derived from and therefore defined by the state, so there is no essential contradiction. More generally Hegel traces the master-slave relationship, showing how individuals are often caught up in conflict based on dominance and submission. Here the master asserts his will on and through the slave, and the slave must carry out the orders of the master. Hegel shows that both figures are diminished in such a dependent relationship because the master is helpless without the slave and the slave has no will of his own. Extrapolating from this, Hegel suggests that every subject must recognize in his object another subjectivity: the object must be as much subject as object. What he is most interested in is the process of manifestation and self-awareness, and here he is very close to Plato and Shakespeare. Just as the individual does not know himself except in the context of the society in which he developed, so qualities do not exist in and of themselves but only in their manifestation in the actions of individuals. Hegel then moves in the opposite direction from Plato. Whereas Plato pursues the essence of qualities in their pure and abstract Forms, Hegel insists that essence must enter the world in action to exist truly.

We therefore see that Shakespeare is closer to Hegel than to Plato, that he seems to present in *Hamlet* and other plays the same sorts of corrections to Plato's metaphysics that Hegel does two hundred years later. Hegel also defines "the beautiful soul" in which we see Hamlet: "It lives in dread of staining the radiance of its inner being by action and existence. And to preserve the purity of its heart, it flees from contact with actuality, and steadfastly persevers in a state of self-willed impotence to renounce a self which is pared away to the last point of abstraction" (VI.C.c., tr. Baillie).

Here we appreciate the contradiction made by serious philosophy to the vulgar notion of philosophy. We might try to reconcile the two according to Platonic or Hegelian dialectic. The vulgar notion of philosophy is that it raises the mind above its circumstances, as in the proposition, "He was philosophical about the death of his father." The suggestion in this statement is that the individual finds some solace in thinking about his father's death as an inevitability of nature or a blessing in disguise (if he did not suffer or if in Christian belief his soul passed on to paradise), or any other way in which he did not dwell on the specificity of his own peculiar loss but saw it rather in the context of the human condition as defined by others. In Hegel we find an insistence that philosophy be used to reintroject the abstract into the specific occurrence, that truth is not a function of removal from the world of experience but rather of revelation here and now.

Hamlet is then, to begin with, philosophical in a Platonic sense but antiphilosophical in a Hegelian sense, and Shakespeare seems determined to show his progress from the one philosopher's position to the other's. Hegel also says, "The individual who has not staked his life may, no doubt, be recognized as a Person; but he has not attained the truth of this recognition as an independent self-consciousness" (233). The relation of one self-consciousness to another is then "a life-and-death struggle." "It is solely by risking life that freedom is obtained; only thus is it tried and proved that the essential nature of self-consciousness is not bare existence." Listen to Hamlet:

> . . . Now whether it be
> Bestial oblivion, or some craven scruple
> Of thinking too precisely on th' event—
> A thought which, quarter'd, hath but one part wisdom
> And ever three parts coward—I do not know
> Why yet I live to say this thing's to do,
> Sith I have cause, and will, and strength, and means
> To do't. (IV.iv.39–46)

Philosophy, then, teaches that philosophy is not enough; the propositions it makes must be tested in the arena of human action. We might say that philosophy by negating philosophy—by taking itself into the world of action—reveals its truth. This prepares us for the fifth act, when Hamlet thrusts himself into the center of court intrigue, which he had always disdained before, and confronts Laertes in the duel—"a life-and-death struggle" wherein his own self-consciousness is finally revealed in confrontation with another self-consciousness. This redeems it from "bare existence," or stupid self-reference. Shakespeare thus actualizes the dynamics of philosophical dialectic. He uses drama to show the gradual drawing out of the philosophical individual into the sphere where the truth of his thinking about himself can be tested. That he dies is, of course, the requirement of tragedy. Recognition comes only with the fall. We know from other contexts that Shakespeare has little respect for the purely ironic individual, who maintains his separation from human action, persisting in his role as uninvolved commentator. This is Jacques in *As You Like It.* Hamlet is different. Having faced death on the voyage to England, he returns with a different perspective, ready now to face death again in order to prove the depth of his self-awareness.

If we look briefly at the twentieth-century philosopher Martin Heidegger, we might convince ourselves that the issues that continue to stimulate philosophical discussion are the very same ones with which Shakespeare confronts Hamlet. Heidegger made the study of Being his focus throughout a long career of teaching and writing. He tried to distinguish his pursuit from that of metaphysicians, by claiming that they were concerned only with the Being of beings, whereas he sought Being itself. Plato thus claimed that the Forms of Truth and Beauty exist absolutely, separate and apart from our immediate experience. Heidegger began his project with the admission that Being must be thought and that the patterns of human thought are revealed in the structure of language; therefore "Language is the house of the truth of Being" ("Letter on Humanism" 193).

Heidegger, like Plato and Hegel—and Shakespeare's Hamlet—seeks in negation the truth of Being, negation being the most radical feature of language. He nostalgically invokes the Greek philosophers before Plato—Parmenides, Heraclitus—convinced that they, for the first and last time, could think and speak Being. Parmenides said that there was only the one path, and that was the path of Being. In this he seems to oppose Heraclitus and other pre-Socratics, such as Empedocles, who saw the world as composed of contradiction, a tension between like and unlike, hot and cold, and so forth. We might trace Plato's Forms to Parmenides, then, in that they are purely positive; the negative in Plato is simply a distance from the positive, not a distinct force of its own. Heidegger tries to distinguish his use of negation from that of previous philosophers. He defines being-in-the-world as *Dasein*, "there-being," and suggests that the only way we can think Being is to think *Dasein* first, with all its temporal determinants, then think the negation of *Dasein* and that is as close as we can come to thinking Being itself.

Death, as the negation of *Dasein*, is as important to Heidegger's thinking of Being, as it is to Hegel, who thinks that the self-consciousness that has not risked death against another self-consciousness has not proved its own independence. Heidegger, seems, though, carefully to contradict Hegel's notion that it takes two self-consciousnesses in contradiction to prove either:

Death is a possibility of Being that each Dasein must itself take over. With death Dasein stands before itself in its most proper potentiality for Being. What is involved in this possibility is nothing less than the being-in-the-world of Dasein as such. Its death is the possibility of being no longer able to be "there." When Dasein stands before itself as this possibility it is fully directed toward its very own potentiality for Being. Standing before itself in this way all relations in it to other Daseins are dissolved. This most proper, nonrelational possibility is at the same time the most extreme. As potentiality for Being, Dasein cannot surmount the possibility of death. Death is the possibility of the unqualified impossibility of Dasein. Death thus reveals itself as the most proper, nonrelational, insurmountable possibility. (*Being and Time* 23)

Heidegger, then, against Hegel, claims that the revelation of the individual's relation to Being can occur in isolation, and not in face of and in contradiction of another. We might think here of Hamlet's isolation at the end of the play. Though he is in conversation with Horatio, we might think of him as thinking out loud to himself, as he does in the soliloquies. "A man's life's but to say 'one.' " At this point, it is not the duel itself that will define Hamlet, but rather his willingness to face death. Laertes is but an excuse; Hamlet must be engaged. He must prove Being by thinking the cancellation of his being-in-the-world.

Recently it has been suggested by a classical scholar studying the relation between fifth-century Greek tragedy and philosophy that tragedy actualizes the theoretical assumptions of philosophy (Nussbaum). We see then that tragedy and philosophy go hand in hand, the one postulating purely logical relations and the other working out these postulations in specific, concrete situations. "Why is it so particular with thee?" Gertrude asks Hamlet. Each person's death is his own, and his preparation for it proves the particularity of his life. Tragedy captures this; philosophy cannot. Philosophy, for all its insistence that we think ourselves through the flotsam and jetsam of ordinary life to some sort of appreciation of our own authenticity—whether in relation to the Forms, the State, or Being—cannot finally arrive there. Its use of language is playful, often ponderous, trying to break down normal expectations to make the revelation of new truth possible. The language of each philosopher can be idiosyncratic, full of neologisms and strange turns of phrase, but it always floats above our own peculiar world. (We need only consider the preponderance of abstract nouns in Plato and Hegel and Heidegger: the Good, Consciousness, Being.) Tragedy, however, especially Shakespeare's tragedy, puts the individual on the stage and isolates him there. He questions his existence in his own peculiar manner. We do not relate to him as a representative of the human condition, but rather to his own uniqueness. He makes us aware of our own uniqueness. Strangely, tragedy—and above all *Hamlet*—takes philosophy beyond itself, forcing it to manifest itself, to prove its own insistence on the individual's isolation.

HAMLET IN THE CONTEXT OF SHAKESPEARE'S OTHER PLAYS

However illustrative and instructive other contexts are—historical, theological, philosophical—the most revealing is Shakespeare's own: his plays illustrate and inform each other. I have already made allusions to other plays to show the persistence of certain themes in the corpus: nominalism in *Romeo and Juliet* and *Henry IV, Part 1*; melancholy in *The Merchant of Venice* and *As You Like It*. Now, I shall show in three constellations of Shakespeare's plays of proximate date with *Hamlet* concerns that we have found essential to *Hamlet*. In *Much Ado About Nothing* (1598), *As You Like It* (1599), and *Othello* (1604), we shall find the problem of perspectivism: each man sees the world in his own unique way. In *Julius Caesar* (1599) and *Troilus and Cressida* (1601), the

reflexivity of self is examined. In three of the four other major tragedies—
Lear (1605), *Macbeth* (1606), and *Coriolanus* (1607)—we find overwhelming female figures who seem to drive the tragic hero to destruction.

In *Much Ado About Nothing* the problem of perspectivism is circumstantial:
Don John causes Claudio "to see" his fiancée, Hero, betray him with another
man on their wedding eve. Precisely the same thing happens in "The Madman
on the Mountain" episode in Cervantes's picaresque novel *Don Quixote*: what
has driven the young man mad is the "scene" of his beloved betraying him on
the day of their wedding. Shakespeare is known to have written a play, now
lost, called *Cardenio*, the name of Cervantes's character. It is a concern, then,
characteristic of his time, but one he made peculiarly his own. In *Othello*, too,
Iago causes Othello to "see and hear" Cassio's boasting of his affair with Desdemona. Othello hides behind a pillar while Iago questions Cassio about his
dalliance with the courtesan Bianca, but Iago has introduced the scene to Othello as an admission of his seduction—and the boredom consequent there-
upon—of Othello's wife. Indeed Shakespeare even uses similar names for the
two villains—Don John and Iago—as he does also for a third, Iacchimo, who
will besmirch the honor of Imogen in the later *Cymbeline*. I have noted that
the science of optics was closely allied with philosophy in the early seventeenth century. Shakespeare himself calls the sudden appearance together
of the twins, Viola and Sebastian, in *Twelfth Night* "a natural perspective"
(V.i.212), to distinguish it from the illusion produced by an optical device.
Descartes warns his reader that the "man" he sees walking before him might
be a robot. Francis Bacon warns about the "idols" of our preconceptions: we
think we know something to be such and such because we have seen or heard
of other such before; this prevents us from judging each circumstance on its
own merits.

Nothing is more characteristic of Shakespeare's age than the attempt to define the self. We have seen how awkward the attempts are in Kyd's *Spanish
Tragedy*, how subtle and complex in *Hamlet*. One might say that this is the
great crisis of the Renaissance: man no longer looks upon himself in relation
to God but rather in relation to other men. By the end of Shakespeare's career,
this High Renaissance humanism had begun to slip from its moorings, and
with such thinkers as Loyola and Southwell we see an attempt to restore the
medieval world order where men subject themselves entirely to the will of
God. Hamlet's dilemma can be seen most precisely as a disjunction between
these two views. In *Julius Caesar* (1599) we hear much of the same language
of the self we do in *Hamlet*. Brutus explains to Cassio his distraction:

> If I have veil'd my look,
> I turn the trouble of my countenance

> Merely upon myself. Vexed I am
> Of late with passions of some difference,
> Conceptions only proper to myself. (I.ii.37–41)

Cassio counsels him:

> And it is very much commented, Brutus,
> That you have no such mirror as will turn
> Your hidden worthiness into your eye. (I.ii.55–57)

Cassio then tempts Brutus:

> I cannot tell what you and other men
> Think of this life; but for my simple self,
> I had as lief not be as live to be
> In awe of such a thing as I myself.
> I was born free as Caesar, so were you. (I.ii.93–97)

This conceit of setting up a mirror to see the self, either within the self or outside in the eyes of others, is behind the doubling in *Hamlet*: he sees himself in Horatio, Laertes, and Fortinbras. We also might hear a hint of his "To be, or not to be," in Cassio's "as lief not be, as live to be."

In *Troilus and Cressida* we find a similar scene. Ulysses, like Hamlet, reading upon a book, baits the arrogant Achilles on the subject of true worth and its appreciation; then Achilles takes the argument further:

Ulysses: A strange fellow here
       Writes me that man, how dearly ever parted,
       How much in having, or without or in,
       Cannot make boast to have that which he hath,
       Nor tells not what he owes, but by reflection;
       As when his virtues, aiming upon others,
       Hears them, and they retort that heat again
       To the first giver.
Achilles: This is not strange, Ulysses,
       The beauty that is borne here in the face
       The bearer knows not, but commends itself
       To others' eyes; nor doth the eye itself,
       Not going from itself, but eye to eye opposed,
       Salutes each other with each other's form;
       For speculation turns not to itself,
       Till it hath travell'd and is mirror'd there
       Where it may see itself. This is not strange at all. (III.iii.95–111)

The strange fellow is Plato, and the text is the obscure, perhaps spurious dialogue "The First Alcibiades," where it is said that only the eye can see another eye, as only the soul can see another soul. Shakespeare probably knew the argument from such Renaissance Platonists as Marsilio Ficino. The complexity comes when one appreciates that it is in the eye of the beholder that one literally sees oneself, reflected as in a mirror—and inverted. The original Greek even employs a suggestive pun: the pupil of the eye is called *korē*, as is also the image of the person looking into the other's eye and seeing himself there. (Latin does the same with *pupilla*, and both words have tertiary meanings of "doll or puppet.") Are we somehow diminished in the eyes of others, captured only there for ourselves to see, but never adequately reflected? We think of Hamlet's reference to Laertes:

I dare not confess that [Laertes's excellence] lest I should compare with him in excellence, but to know a man well were to know himself. (V.ii.137–139)

Can any man know any other man, or only himself, and can he know himself only in relation to another man? We shall see in Chapter 6 that the psychoanalyst and philosopher Jacques Lacan poses the same problem with his trope on *méconnaissance*: if we know ourselves only in our relations with others, then our knowledge of ourselves is false. More profoundly, in *Hamlet*, is there a type of man to which all examples are subjected, or are there only examples, each unique? If the idea of man has taken the place of God in Renaissance thinking, then Shakespeare calls it into question, and with it Truth and the nature of Being.

Finally let us look at the figure of Gertrude in Hamlet's imagination and compare her with Lady Macbeth, Goneril and Regan, and Volumnia. He sees her as something "rank and gross in nature . . . an unweeded garden." This image of the mature woman as sexually insatiable is a constant in Shakespeare; in the mature tragedies, it becomes an obsession. Shakespeare devotes a whole scene to Hamlet's abuse of his mother (the closet scene, III.iv), and we shall return in Chapter 5 to the attempt to integrate this misogyny with other aspects of his thinking. Here we need only recognize the same male nightmare fantasy of the sexually insatiable woman in *Lear*, *Macbeth*, and *Coriolanus*.

Lear, driven mad by his rapacious daughters, identifies all the evils of the world with woman's sexuality and her hypocritical cover for it:

> Behold yon simpr'ing dame,
> Whose face between her forks presages snow,
> That minces virtue, and does shake the head

To hear of pleasure's name—
The fitchew nor the soiled horse goes to 't
With a more riotous appetite.
Down from the waist they are Centaurs,
Though women all above;
But to the girdle do the gods inherit,
Beneath is all the fiends': there's hell, there's darkness,
There is the sulphrous pit, burning, scalding,
Stench, consumption. Fie, fie, fie! pah, pah! (IV.vi.118–28)

In *Coriolanus* Shakespeare takes the hero's mother's name Volumnia, and turns her into the personification of the overwhelming mother. The play is conceived around a central image of feeding—Menenius tells the people that the senators are the belly and they the various extremities of the body: the senate must ingest all wealth and distribute it to the others—and Volumnia constantly refers to her body as the source not of sustenance but of violence:

I sprang not more in joy at first hearing he was a man-child
than now in seeing he had prov'd himself a man. (I.iii.15–17)

... The breasts of Hecuba,
When she did suckle Hector, look'd not lovelier
Than Hector's forehead when it spat forth blood
At Grecian sword contemning! (I.iii.40–43)

Thy valiantness was mine, thou suck'st it from me;
But owe thy pride thyself. (III.ii.128–29)

Anger's my meat; I sup upon myself,
And so shall starve with feeding. (IV.ii.50–51)

... thou shalt no sooner
March to assault thy country than to tread
(Trust to 't, thou shalt not) on thy mother's womb
That brought thee to this world. (V.iii.122–24)

It is probably the same argument—and the same obsession with the mother's nursing turned to violence—that characterizes the relations between Lady Macbeth and Macbeth. She fears that he is "too full of the milk of human kindness" to act on his ambition to usurp the throne from Duncan. She constantly questions his manhood and claims that it is only she who can instill manliness in him:

> . . . Come to my women's breasts,
> And take my milk for gall, you murth'ring ministers,
> Wherever in your sightless substances
> You wait on nature's mischief! (I.v.47–52)

> . . . I have given suck, and know
> How tender 'tis to love the babe that milks me;
> I would, while it was smiling in my face,
> Have pluck'd my nipple from his boneless gums
> And dash'd the brains out, had I so sworn as you
> Have done to this. (I.vii.54–59)

In the comedies women are seen only, mistakenly, to be evil, but in the tragedies Shakespeare puts the monsters before our eyes. Gertrude is a transitional figure: Hamlet sees her as much worse than she is. Indeed her complexity is precisely in the contradictions between what she has done and what he thinks she has done. Did she commit adultery with Claudius before her husband's death? Did she know of the murder? Hamlet thinks that all the horrors of incest and fratricide spring from her ungovernable lust. In fact she is not Goneril or Regan or Lady Macbeth. She is not even the kind of domineering monster of a mother that Volumnia is.

Hamlet's reconciliation with his mother at the end of the closet scene and in the dueling scene at the end of the play shows his acceptance of her reality as different from his vile imaginings. He wakes from his nightmare of misogyny just as he has already waked from his nightmare of eternal torment in hell. To see Shakespeare's treatment of these themes and developments across the whole corpus of his work is extremely revealing. Male characters define themselves, in and of themselves, in their relations with other men and in their wild imaginings of what women expect of them. In this last case there is nothing there, and it is that void which the man strives to fill.

3

DRAMATIC STRUCTURE

Some of the distinctions critics usually make in discussing drama do not apply to Shakespeare, especially not to *Hamlet*. Aristotle insists on the importance of action over character: "one can have tragedy without character, but no tragedy without action" (*Poetics* 1450a). In *Hamlet* the structure of the action—how the plot develops from scene to scene and act to act—is determined by the development of Hamlet's character. So, too, in speaking of the language of drama, Aristotle suggests that it be appropriate to the thought. In Shakespeare, however, language and thought are organically whole, the development of an image often determining the development of a theme.

The great soliloquies in *Hamlet* are not interruptions to the movement of the plot or artificial encumbrances, but rather the structural highlights of each major unit of action. Hamlet as a character must reveal what is hidden, so the plot of *Hamlet* is a gradual revelation of what is rotten in the state of Denmark, and the soliloquies tell us how Hamlet thinks and feels about this. The soliloquies are like arias in modern opera. The action has moved forward in duets and other exchanges between characters, but in the aria, a major character expresses his or her emotional response to all this. The two great polarities in *Hamlet* are between appearance and reality (or the seen and the unseen) and between intention and accomplishment. Hamlet's notorious hesitation is a function of his seeing his circumstances more clearly and meditating on their significance more profoundly. He is disgusted by the world he lives in but is not immediately convinced that changing it is worth his while:

> The time is out of joint: O cursed spite,
> That ever I was born to set it right! (I.v.188–89)

Language is a revelation of both thought and character. In Shakespeare more than in any other dramatist, language is appropriate to the character speaking, and in *Hamlet* it has been shown that Hamlet speaks in more than one style. All characters use elaborate rhetorical figures, and Hamlet is the most elaborate of them all, but these are not mere decorations. What Hamlet thinks and feels can be expressed only in the words he chooses since the patterns of his thinking are so complex that simple expression would distort them. So, too, with the intricate imagery. Constant reference is made to what is natural and unnatural, what is pure and what corrupt, what is fresh and what decayed. Hamlet's whole conception of the world seems to be based on a horticultural analogy (which, again, is essentially Aristotelian): there is youth-and-beauty, but then there is decay-and-death. We can trace this back to earlier works. It is especially prominent in *Romeo and Juliet* and the *Sonnets* (which might well be contemporary with *Hamlet*). But in *Hamlet* it becomes obsessive. He begins by seeing his mother's body as something rank and gross in nature, but then all of nature—the world entire—becomes infected.

Hamlet's use of puns is proverbial; he is Renaissance wit personified. But whereas in other plays—in the mouths of other characters—such word play can be tedious, with Hamlet it is revealing. We might compare him with Mercutio in *Romeo and Juliet*: both are bawdy and outrageous, their energy driving them beyond normal linguistic bounds, and both are death-directed, seeming to explode almost physically before us as their verbal fireworks go off in our ears. Mercutio puns on erotic terms:

> If love be rough with you, be rough with love;
> Prick love for pricking, and you beat love down. (I.iv.27–28)

Hamlet does likewise, in commenting on the play within the play for Ophelia:

Ophelia: You are as good as a chorus, my lord.

Hamlet: I could interpret between you and your love,
    If I could see the puppets dallying.

Ophelia: You are keen, my lord, you are keen.

Hamlet: It would cost you a groaning to take off mine edge. (III.ii.345–348)

Mercutio receives a fatal sword thrust that Romeo says "cannot be much":

No, 'tis not so deep as a well, nor so wide as a church-door, but 'tis enough, 'twill serve. Ask for me tomorrow and you will find me a grave man. (III.i.95–98)

Hamlet taunts Polonius, who then uses the polite phrase, "My lord, I will take my leave of you." Hamlet replies:

You cannot take from me anything that I will not more willingly part withal—except my life, except my life, except my life. (II.ii.214–16)

Why is the truth so often said in jest? Normal people, like Polonius and Osric, might struggle to find a pleasing way to say something, a complicated way to say a simple thing, but Hamlet thinks aloud in language. Freud has shown us how verbal wit releases repressed energy, and "serious jokes"—those about sex and death—bring on the most convulsive laughter. Hamlet, like Mercutio, often runs out of control. Like a schizophrenic, he does not attempt to fit his language to the reality of the world, because he is outside and beyond that world. He creates another world out of language that is sharper, clearer, closer to the truth.

ACTION AND CHARACTER

Modern editions of *Hamlet* divide the play into acts and scenes, following the divisions in the First Folio; the two Quartos lack these. (The First Folio divides only the first two acts; late-seventeenth-century editors extended the practice through the rest of the play.) It is disputed whether they were part of Shakespeare's intention, and whether they indicate breaks in performance on the Globe stage. On the latter question it is helpful to remember that sharp distinction between scenes is a feature of modern theatre, where curtains can drop and lights can dim. In the open-air Globe, where the playing space thrust out into the audience, this was impossible. There is every reason to believe that action was continuous in the early performances; indeed in most performances now, that is the rule. Only in productions where the scenery takes precedence over the actors do we see literal scene changes. There is a discernible rhythm in the action of Shakespeare's plays, which becomes palpable in sensitive productions. A meditative moment is broken up by the entry of revelers, or a stately procession passes and one character is left alone on stage.

This represents an entirely different view of how time passes and how our actions are related to one another in sequence and simultaneously with other action taking place elsewhere (i.e., "another part of the forest"). On the proscenium stage, there is a kind of self-conscious realism. We are asked to look in on the actors as if the fourth wall of a room were transparent. Then, as if we were not able to tell when time has passed between moments of action, the curtain descends and rises again as a clue. This was taken over into early film with the flash card, "And, the next day . . ." held up to the camera, or a blackout on the screen, or, for longer gaps, the headlines of newspapers flashing by or the pages of a calendar. Shakespeare clearly had a different conception of time and how events succeed and alter each other. Action moves forward in dialogue scenes (it is decided that Hamlet must be sent to England), but in the soliloquies, time stands still, and the significance of action is questioned. If we ever have the illusion that we are at Elsinore overhearing Hamlet speak to himself, then this is accomplished through his words, not through a change of scene. In the Globe Theatre the actor would have moved forward on the stage so as to approach the center of the audience, and spoken his lines in a changed tone.

It has been suggested that in *Hamlet*, at least, Shakespeare attempted to please "the wiser sort"—those familiar with scholarly commentary on ancient Greek and Roman tragedy (Melchiori). The First Quarto specifies that the play had been "diverse times acted" at Oxford and Cambridge. There a tradition had arisen in the mid-sixteenth century of acting out imitations of classical drama. In Greek tragedy of the fifth century B.C., there were no divisions into acts and scenes; the action on stage was continuous. There were, however, alternations between spoken and sung passages, which gave the performances rhythm and structure.

Generally the play would open with a monologue or dialogue spoken by an actor on stage, and this would be followed by the entrance of the chorus, who sang and danced in the space slightly below and before the stage (the orchestra, or "dancing space"). The action would move forward in the dialogue sections (*epeisodia*, because they came in between the "odes" of the chorus), and then the chorus would meditate in song on the significance of that action as they moved about in the orchestra. This all became regularized in the tragedies of the Roman poet and philosopher Seneca in the first century A.D. These plays were probably never acted out but only read aloud. They contain four choruses; hence the division of the action into five "acts." There is a similar development in ancient comedy. In the fifth-century B.C. comedies of Aristophanes, the divisions are intricate and traditional. There are dialogue portions, but then elaborate choral intrusions, such as when the chorus divides and debates among themselves, and when they address the audience directly. In the fourth-century B.C. comedy of Menander, the chorus has been reduced to a horde of drunken revelers who stumble onto the stage at four intervals. Their songs have not survived, but only the notation *chorou*, "[entrance] of the chorus." It was the plays of Menander and his contemporary playwrights Diphilos and Philemon that furnished the originals for the Latin adaptations of Plautus and Terence in the second century B.C. These were known to Shakespeare, as were the tragedies of Seneca.

Although action on both the Greek and Roman stages in both comedy and tragedy was continuous, the convention arose in late antiquity of dividing the plays into acts and scenes. The rubrics were simple: scene divisions meant the entrance of a new character; act divisions meant an empty stage. These seemingly insignificant designations can conceal important structural principles. For instance, insofar as the act divisions in a play by Terence reveal the choral interludes in the original play by Menander, they mark important stages in the development of the action. It has been shown (Handley) that Menander built up his action in precise and intricate units. Each interval of dialogue would reach a climax just a few lines before the entrance of the chorus, and then that interval would end with the entrance of a new character or the revelation of some new piece of information. In the fourth interval, the essential problem of the play would be solved—the young girl who was thought to be a slave and thus doomed to lead a life of prostitution is recognized as the lost daughter of the man next door, so she can marry the young man who loves her—and then the interval after the last choral interlude would be devoted to tying up loose ends. Thus the structure of the play as a whole—climax before conclusion, then starting up again—is reflected in each of the constituent "acts."

Technical terms became attached to the various traditional elements of the action of both tragedy and comedy. Aristotle, writing late in the fourth century B.C., found in Greek tragedy of the fifth century essential patterns of *dēsis* and *lusis* ("complication" and "resolution," respectively), *peripeteia* and *anagnōrisis* ("turn about in fortune" and "recognition," respectively). In the scholarly tradition following Aristotle, and known to Shakespeare's contemporaries at the universities, other terms were added to the discussion of tragedy, although they had originally been restricted to comedy. The action was expected to be divided into the *protasis* ("preparation" or "that which comes before necessitating all that follows") of the first three acts, *epitasis* ("development"), and *catastasis* ("complication" in the action, when its significance is questioned") in the fourth, and *catastrophe* ("disastrous reversal") in the fifth. Melchiori argues that Shakespeare structured *Hamlet* to meet these expectations. The crux of his argument is that the fourth act soliloquy, "How all occasions do inform against me," is a perfect *catastasis*, and it is found only in the fuller, more "scholarly" Second Quarto (along with the consideration of Aristotle's concept of *hamartia*—"tragic flaw"—in the "mole of nature" speech of I.v).

We are asked to consider, then, various determinations for the sequence of the action in *Hamlet*. Shakespeare had developed his extraordinary skill at structuring action into significant units and subordinating these to an overarching argument in the ten years of his playwrighting that led up to *Hamlet*. Most apposite is his shaping of the episodic material of Holinshed's *Chronicles* into the coherently dramatized narratives of the early history plays. Also comparable is adaptation of the endlessly episodic Italian romances for the early comedies. These skills we might relate, to some extent, to his reading of and adapting classical drama (e.g. *The Comedy of Errors*, based on Plautus's *Menaechmi*). (Miola finds precise and pervasive influence of Platus and Terence even on *Hamlet* 174–86.) Then there was the shape of the revenge play, specifically the *Ur-Hamlet*: the expectation would be built up to the consummation of revenge, but then, as in *The Spanish Tragedy*, there is delay and self-doubt. Finally we must consider the suggestion that Shakespeare made an effort in *Hamlet* to formulate a new and different form of drama. Supporting this are the extraordinary length of the play, its references to Aristotle, its departure from his previous attempts at tragedy (*Titus Andronicus, Romeo and Juliet, Julius Caesar*), and, most important, as Melchiori points out, the introspective quality of the play. He insists that unlike other revenge plays, Hamlet is concerned with "inquest rather than conquest" (196–97). Other critics have also seen in *Hamlet* a departure. Bloom finds in Hamlet the first character in the tradtion of drama to develop in the course of his own play (ix–xiv). Clearly the development of Hamlet's character is the basis on which the action of the play is structured. We should therefore examine the structure of the play as a revelation of character. This will congrue with our other discusssions of Renaissance subjectivity and Shakespeare's notions of man in relation to nature, to other men, and to himself.

The greatest contrast in the play is between illusion and reality, or between what is accepted by others but rejected by Hamlet, or—most philosophically—between what actually happens and what it ultimately means. If we take the soliloquies as punctuating the action of the play the way the choral interludes do in Greek drama, then we see that its basic structure is determined by its basic theme. In the soliloquies the action comes to a halt, and its significance is questioned. Indeed, notoriously, the question posed in the soliloquies is whether any action is worth taking, whether anything is worth doing. This note of skepticism is first struck by Horatio in the opening scene. He doubts the sentries' report of a ghost walking on the ramparts. Then, immediately, when the Ghost appears, it is described as "like the King . . . ? Most like . . . As thou art to thyself" (I.i.46–62). Finally, Horatio interprets the Ghost's appearance as an omen: "This bodes some strange eruption to our state" (72). Thus appearances must be interpreted; nothing should be taken at face value. This theme is developed in the following scene, when Hamlet protests against Claudius's calling him son: "A little more than kin and less than kind" (I.ii.65). He puns here on the word "kind," which can mean both "considerate" and "like": "you might be twice related to me, but you are nothing like me." Hamlet then pursues the difference between seeming and being in response to his mother's question about why grief "seems so particular" with him:

> Seems, madam? Nay, it is. I know not "seems."
> 'Tis not alone my inky cloak, good mother,
> Nor customary suits of solemn black,
> Nor windy suspiration of forc'd breath,
> No, nor the fruitful river in the eye,
> Nor the dejected haviour of the visage,
> Together with all forms, moods, shapes of grief,

That can denote me truly. These indeed seem,
For they are actions that a man might play;
But I have that within which passes show,
These but the trappings and the suits of woe. (76–86)

The contrasts here are between surface appearance and inner reality, assumed role and actual emotional state; this will become crucial as the play progresses and Hamlet's character develops. He will convince us that he lives life differently from others, that he seeks the hidden truth. We might recall the insistence in Saxo Grammaticus that Amleth was the "truth-teller," that he could fathom the mystery of situations and describe them accurately, though in riddling language.

With the preparation of these two scenes—the first on the ramparts, the second in the court—we arrive at the first soliloquy, "O that this too too sullied flesh would melt" (I.ii.129–58). The points to be made in this consideration of the play's structure are how it relates to the opening scenes and develops the themes there introduced.

Hamlet first expresses a generalized *taedium vitae*, but he goes on to specify his mother's infidelity as its cause: "How weary, stale, flat, and unprofitable / *Seem* to me all the uses of this world!" (133–34); "Frailty, thy name is woman" (146). The transition from melancholy to misogyny comes in the comparison of his father with his uncle: "Hyperion to a satyr" (140), "My father's brother—but no more like my father / Than I to Hercules" (152–53). She only seemed to love his father; she only seemed to be a chaste woman; she only seemed to be in control of her desires. In fact, she is bestial in her appetites. Hamlet thus interprets his mother the way Horatio interprets the Ghost, as an omen: "It is not, nor it cannot come to good" (158). This first sequence of action comes to a climax with the revelation of a hidden reality. As Melchiori puts it, the play is about inquest rather than conquest. The greatest insights are reached in the soliloquies; it is there that the cloud of illusion is penetrated, the curtain lifted, and the truth revealed.

After his soliloquy, Hamlet is joined by Horatio, Marcellus, and Bernardo, who inform him of the ghost's appearance. The subject is introduced with a turn of phrase that continues and deepens previous concerns:

Hamlet: My father—methinks I see my father—

Horatio: Where, my lord?

Hamlet: In my mind's eye, Horatio.

Horatio: I saw him once; a was a goodly king.

Hamlet: A was a man, take him for all in all:
I shall not look upon his like again. (I.ii.184–88)

Horatio has used the expression "in the mind's eye" already, to suggest the power of imagination as opposed to the visual sense (I.i.115); here Hamlet's use suggests his distraction: he is still absorbed in the considerations of his soliloquy. Hence he continues to be obsessed with the difference between Claudius and his father. When he first sees Horatio, he exclaims, "Horatio, or I do forget myself" (161). This is both a figure of speech and a strong, literal statement: he considers Horatio his alter ego. He then goes on to lament the close conjunction of his father's death and his mother's remarriage and then to state what first appears to be the praise appropriate for a son of his father, but we realize it is also a philosophical statement: because he was a man, he was unique. Horatio's description of the Ghost's appearance ends with the lines: "I knew your father; / These hands are not more like" (211–12). The implication is that though each man is unique and unexampled in this life, some image of him persists in the next. The transition from Hamlet's mental image of his father to Horatio's sighting of the Ghost forces us to connect the two. Later we will also connect the notion that a man has an image of himself that sustains him in the intervals between his mirroring of himself in his contacts with others. These are the moments of the soliloquies.

There is no subplot in *Hamlet*; rather Shakespeare introduces us into the domestic affairs of another family besides the royals, the family of the courtier Polonius. We have already met the son, Laertes, and seen the comparison and contrast with Hamlet: he has requested permission to return to his studies in Paris, though Hamlet is persuaded not to return to his in Wittenberg. Now, in Act I, scene iii, his father gives him moral advice, culminating in the pregnant phrase, "To thine own self be true" (78). We also meet Polonius's daughter, Ophelia, and learn that Hamlet has made romantic overtures to her. Her father and brother both discourage her from receiving such attention: this introduces the theme of sexual repression, which will later lead to her madness and death. Her father will consistently maintain that it is Hamlet's unrequited love for her that drives him mad. Thus Hamlet and Ophelia are joined in a cruel contrast: his madness is both feigned and real, the latter brought on by the death of his father and his mother's overhasty marriage; Ophelia will actually go mad when Hamlet kills her father, and her madness will be characterized by the singing of bawdy songs. Both Hamlet and Ophelia will be credited with revealing truths in their madness that sane people do not see. The large themes associated, then, are the deaths of fathers, the relations between madness and sexuality, and the revelation of truth in madness. Clearly all of these are related to the largest theme, the individual's hidden identity.

For the last two scenes of Act I, we return to the ramparts. At the beginning of this sequence—but only in the Second Quarto—Hamlet delivers the long speech on the "mole of nature" (I.iv.14–38). The sequence of its thought is this: Danes drink too much, and this spoils their reputation abroad; individual men have peculiar faults, and this ruins their reputations. Then the Ghost appears. What is the connection? The speech is a private meditation, like a soliloquy, but here it is spoken in the company of others. Shakespeare raises the question whether a man is such and such by nature or by reputation. In Aristotle the "tragic flaw" is *hamartia*, and critics continue to debate what precisely he means by it. Technically it should mean a mistake of judgment, "missing the mark." However, the way he uses it and the fact that he uses it of Oedipus in Sophocles' play suggests rather that it is an aspect of character— that certain men characteristically make certain mistakes. Hamlet is then thinking about the hidden flaws in men, and especially about Claudius, since he is the one who called for the drunken revel, when the Ghost appears to reveal the hidden truth of his death: Claudius seduced his wife and killed him. (This is the order of events in the Ghost's report; it is consistent with Hamlet's abuse of his mother in III.iv, but not with the play within the play in III.ii.) The act ends with Hamlet's assumption of an "antic disposition." He has realized that one may "smile and smile and be a villain." He has also corrected his friend's skepticism: "There are more things, Horatio, / Than are dreamt of in your philosophy" (174–75). Claudius is a villain but a hypocrite; to seek his vengeance, Hamlet himself will have to pretend to be what he is not: mad.

What does the act break here signify? Most obviously it marks the passage of time: "Laertes has time to settle in Paris, Hamlet to show in full his antic disposition, Rosencrantz and Guildenstern to be recalled to Elsinore and the ambassadors to go and return from Norway" (Melchiori 197). We certainly see the shape of the first act: the Ghost appears in the first and last scenes to make his demand. He has risen up from the earth to confirm his son's worst suspicions and to demand of him action. It is not unlike the plague in Sophocles' *Oedipus Tyrannos*: the murderer of Laios has gone unpunished all these years, but the plague now demands that he be found. The irony that Oedipus, as king, takes on the responsibility of punishing the murderer, who is he himself, is not without parallel in *Hamlet*. In pursuing—and not pursuing— vengeance for his father's murder, Hamlet "finds himself." His last thought in Act I is characterizing: "The time is out of joint. O cursed spite, / That ever I was born to set it right" (196–97). Circumstances beyond his control will force him to act in an uncharacteristic manner. Nothing could be more dramatic, more tragic. The conflict is not between two individuals but within one, or between what he knows of himself in the private world of his own meditation and the public role he must now assume. The assumption of the role of a madman is metaphorical as well as an aspect of the plot: it suggests Shakespeare's primary philosophical concern, which is the nature of individual identity and how it is and is not manifest in behavior with others.

The second act begins with the first of several important spying scenes (II.i): Polonius sends Reynaldo to spy on Laertes in Paris; then Ophelia reports that Hamlet has appeared to her "As if he had been loosed out of hell, / To speak of horrors" (83–84). This confirms Polonius in the opinion that Hamlet's madness is the result of unrequited love. Act II, scene ii is another spying scene: Rosencrantz and Guildenstern have returned to Elsinore at Claudius's request, and they are set to spy on Hamlet, to find out the cause of his "transformation." Claudius specifies that neither "the exterior nor the inward man / Resembles that it was" (6–7). Rosencrantz and Guildenstern reply: "But we both obey, / And here give up ourselves in the full bent / To lay our service freely at your feet / To be commanded" (29–32). They then join with Hamlet and Horatio and Polonius in the reflexive use of "self" compounds; in their case, one wonders what their "selves" consist of. Claudius and Gertrude seem even to confuse them:

King: Thanks, Rosencrantz and gentle Guildenstern.
Queen: Thanks Guildenstern and gentle Rosencrantz. (33–34)

The other pair of indistinguishable courtiers, Cornelius and Voltemand, then report to the king on their embassy to Norway. When they depart, Polonius presents to Claudius and Gertrude his hypothesis that Hamlet's madness is caused by unrequited love of Ophelia, which he is determined to prove:

> If circumstance lead me, I will find
> Where truth is hid, though it were hid indeed
> Within the centre. (157–59)

Hamlet enters reading on a book, and Polonius interrogates him. Polonius comments on his riddling answers: "Though this be madness, yet there is method in't" (205). The impression grows apace that the world is mad, and only Hamlet has insight into it. (We might compare Bottom's dream in *A Midsummer Night's Dream*: being loved by the fairy queen Titania is like Hamlet's being visited by his father's ghost: it is the revelation of truth from another realm and difficult to share with those who have not been similarly visited.)

The scene continues with the first interview between Hamlet and Rosencrantz/Guildenstern. Hamlet calls Denmark a prison, and they dispute with him. He concludes: "For there is nothing either good or bad but thinking makes it so" (250). Like so many other lines in the play touching on the nature of reality and man's perception of it (i.e., truth), this line is open to a range of interpretations. At the very least it suggests a philosophical relativism not unlike Hobbes's: there are no absolute values, but each individual is driven by his own attractions and aversions. More radically, and in keeping with Hamlet's role as the madman who speaks the truth—Theseus says the imagination of the lunatic, like that of the lover and the poet (Hamlet is all three), "gives to airy nothing a local habitation and a name"—it can be read as doubting existence itself: nothing exists, whether good or bad, but for the thinking of it. It is important to note that in what follows, Hamlet first forces from his two false friends the confession that they were sent for to spy on him, before he delivers his famous speech on his melancholy: "I have of late, but wherefore I know not, lost all my mirth" (295–96). It is, then, for their benefit, to mislead them from the real cause of his despair: the knowledge of his father's murder. Again, it is a speech like a soliloquy, in that it is meditative, but being spoken in the company of known spies, it is disingenuous. This is extremely important, as it might prepare us for another passage of similar difficulty: "To be, or not to be."

Rosencrantz and Guildenstern announce the arrival of the players, and Hamlet immediately connects the world of the stage with the world of the court: "He that plays the king shall be welcome" (318). He elsewhere calls Claudius a "king of shreds and patches," which might suggest the motley of theatrical costume. The usurper is like the actor; he assumes a role not rightly his. The world is a theatre in which we play our assigned roles, or take on others, or refuse to play altogether. Hamlet has so far refused the role of avenger. He has assumed the role of the madman; now he seems to slip into the world of the theatre altogether, more competent there to write his own part than to act out his assigned role. The juxtaposition of the arrival of the players on the pregnant phrase, "nothing is . . . but thinking makes it so," calls into question the nature of reality and puts the artist in control of lived experience. This comes to a climax with the great soliloquy that ends the act, "O what a rogue and peasant slave am I!" (544–601).

The First Player, at Hamlet's request, has recited a description of the Fall of Troy, focusing on the murder of King Priam by Achilles' son Pyrrhus. The situation described is then a remote parallel to Hamlet's own: Pyrrhus is an extreme case of the vengeful son, running beserk and killing the old king in front of his horrified wife, Hecuba. (In Book II of Virgil's *Aeneid*, the ultimate source of the scene, Pyrrhus first kills Priam's son Polites, and then the old man, slipping in his own son's blood; as vengeance, it is indirect, since it was another of Priam's sons, Paris, who had killed Pyrrhus's father, Achilles.) When the First Player comes to the part about Hecuba's grief, he breaks off in tears. It is this response to an old tale that causes Hamlet to compare his own case to that of the player:

> Is it not monstrous that this player here,
> But in a fiction, in a dream of passion,

> Could force his soul so to his own conceit
> That from her working all his visage wann'd,
> Tears in his eyes, distraction in his aspect,
> A broken voice, and his whole function suiting
> With forms to his conceit? And all for nothing!
> For Hecuba!
> What's Hecuba to him, or he to her,
> That he should weep for her? What would he do
> Had he the motive and the cue for passion
> That I have? (545–56)

"And all for nothing" reminds us of "there is nothing either good or bad but thinking makes it so." In both cases something is made up out of nothing. Though there is some contrast between "thinking" and "a dream of passion" (i.e., between the intellectual and the emotional), essentially both passages deal with affect—the response of the individual to his circumstances. The second passage is more precise: the player first conceives of the effect he would like to create in his audience and then forces his soul to take that impression so that through its perturbation ("her working") he pales, he weeps, he gestures wildly and stammers. In the rest of his long speech, Hamlet berates himself, unleashing upon himself that fury that in the first soliloquy he had spent on his mother. Again he compares his worthy father to his uncle: "Bloody, bawdy villain! / Remorseless, treacherous, lecherous, kindless villain!" ("Kindless" reminds us of "A little more than kin and less than kind"; here it means both "unnatural" and "without parallel.") Now he is a coward, behaving "like a whore," all words and no deeds. Then he develops the plan he had already conceived: the players will perform *The Murder of Gonzago*, a play that will shock Claudius with its resemblance to his own crime: "The play's the thing / Wherein I'll catch the conscience of the King."

The act break here is appropriate. First, time passes—overnight—so that the players can prepare. Then, too, in those terms, perhaps originally Aristotelian, applied by Renaissance scholars to dramatic texts, the *protasis*, or preparation of the play, is complete, and we are now in the *epitasis*, or development stage, where complications are introduced. Also, in the relation between plot and character, Hamlet seems now about to reveal what he knows: Claudius's guilt. Why, then, fifty-six lines into the third act, do we hear another soliloquy, the most memorable of them all, "To be, or not to be"? In the First Quarto, the sequence of scenes found in other editions at the opening of Act III follows immediately upon Polonius's original suggestion early in Act II, scene ii, before the arrival of the players, that he set up an interview between Hamlet and his daughter. In terms of both character and plot, it would seem to fit better there; the arrival of the players has not yet given him the plan to expose the king's guilt, and his anxiety over the Ghost's injunction to revenge might well have induced thoughts of suicide. In the Second Quarto and First Folio, the sequence of action in Act II, scene iii is brief: exchange between king, queen, and Rosencrantz/Guildenstern, followed by the king and Polonius's positioning themselves behind the curtain; "To be, or not to be"; nunnery scene. This is extremely awkward. Why must the speech traditionally taken as Hamlet's most profound self-scrutiny be sandwiched between two elements of a spying scene, which is engineered only to prove Polonius's false contention that Hamlet's madness was brought on by his unrequited love of Ophelia?

An examination of the soliloquy might help answer this question. It opens with the phrase that has generally been taken as a consideration of suicide—though we have seen in another context that there are alternative interpretations—and continues with a contrast between the vagaries of life and the surcease of care in death: "The slings and arrows of outrageous fortune / . . . a consummation / Devoutly to be wished." Then comes a catalog of life's abuses, but also a fear of punishment after death. The end of the speech is ambiguous:

> Thus conscience does make cowards of us all,
> And thus the native hue of resolution
> Is sicklied o'er with the pale cast of thought,
> And enterprises of great pitch and moment
> With this regard their currents turn awry
> And lose the name of action. (83–88)

How can suicide be considered an enterprise "of great pitch and moment"? While it is true that suicide is treated in the opening lines as a heroic act—"to take arms against a sea of troubles"—it seems that by the end of the speech, Hamlet has moved from thoughts of killing himself to thoughts of killing Claudius. (In Christian belief—more pronounced in Catholic than in Protestant—suicide is as damnable a sin as murder.) The most salient feature of this soliloquy is its generalized, philosophical orientation. Hamlet does not refer to any of the peculiarities of his own case; there is nothing about his father, his mother, or his uncle, the focuses of the previous two soliloquies. The speech that this soliloquy most resembles is that delivered to Rosencrantz and Guildenstern: "I have of late, but wherefore I know not, lost all my mirth" (II.ii.295–310). Hamlet already knows they "were sent for" when he delivers it. We must at least consider the possibility that "To be, or not to be" is similarly contextual. It is delivered with the knowledge that Claudius and Polonius are listening; it is another attempt by Hamlet to give the impression of a generalized melancholy rather than a specific anxiety over revenge. (The only other tragedy similarly punctuated by soliloquies is *Macbeth*, and there the general is mixed consistently with the specific.)

In performance various ploys have been used to overcome the awkwardness felt here. Olivier takes Hamlet up to the ramparts to deliver "To be, or not to be," and then has him abuse Ophelia in the nunnery scene because he sees Claudius and Polonius position themselves behind the curtain. Ralph Fiennes delivered "To be, or not to be" at an unnaturally swift pace, either to acknowledge that it has become a cliché, or to suggest that Hamlet is giving only perfunctory attention to the conventions of melancholy (for the benefit of the eavesdroppers). Another, even more complex consideration is that Shakespeare here brings feigned madness and genuine madness into the same moment: Hamlet says what Claudius and Polonius expect to hear but also means it—that the only meaningful action is taken in the face of death. Only thus are we prepared for the about-face of the graveyard scene later—and his preparation for the duel—when he renounces all fear of death. There is also poignancy in Ophelia's overhearing of this talk of suicide, since that is the interpretation put upon her death, though the way Gertrude describes it, she drowned accidentally while following the dictates of her madness.

How do these considerations affect our notion of the structure of this opening sequence of Act III? We have so far contrasted the soliloquies to the dialogue portions of the play as meditation on completed action. Each of the first two soliloquies is a response to new circumstance and a prediction of what is to come; this soliloquy is neither. It stands out from the action, even contradicting the determination Hamlet has expressed at the end of the previous act and arresting the momentum toward the confrontation with Claudius in the play scene. At the end of the nunnery scene, however, Claudius announces his interpretation of Hamlet's state of mind—"Love? His affections do not that way tend, / Nor what he spake, though it lack'd form a little, / Was not like madness" (164–66)—and determines to send him to England; Polonius adds the suggestion that his mother speak to him. (Polonius himself will overhear—another spying scene.) The next scene opens with Hamlet's instructing the players.

The forty-five-line sequence is an almost uninterrupted disquisition on the art of acting; one wonders whether Hamlet is not here commenting on his own just completed performance. His emphasis is on naturalism, and the center of his discussion is the Aristotelian concept of art as imitation (*mimesis*) of nature.

Suit the action to the word, the word to the action, with this special observance, that you o'erstep not the modesty of nature. For anything so o'erdone is from the purpose of playing, whose end, both at the first and now, was and is to hold as 'twere the mirror up to nature; to show virtue her feature, scorn her own image, and the very age and body of the time his form and pressure. (17–24)

There are constant references to nature throughout the play: the death of fathers is natural, his mother's behavior is unnatural, if nature is in him he will avenge his father's murder. Here he points to a standard of human behavior that actors must approximate. We recall from his second soliloquy that actors can identify with their roles to such an extent that appearance and demeanor alters, as we would say, unconsciously. Hamlet's purpose is to elicit an emotional response from Claudius to *The Murder of Gonzago*. The actors must then give the illusion that the murder is actually taking place. Then the intended moral effect will be achieved: "to show virtue her feature, scorn her own image, and the very age and body of the time his form and pressure." Art can reveal truth and therefore change character, or at least behavior. (This, like the division of the drama into *protasis, epitasis*, and *catastrophe*, is traceable back to commentaries from late antiquity on the comedies of Terence, and beyond to the lost second book of Aristotle's *Poetics*, perhaps preserved for us in the medieval *Tractatus Coislinianus*.) It has a moral function.

This piece of dramatic criticism is immediately followed by Hamlet's praise of Horatio for not being a hypocrite, like the other members of the court; we think specifically of Rosencrantz and Guildenstern. This is the heart of Hamlet's irony. He is himself a consummate actor (*hypokrites*), but abhors those who assume roles either unconsciously or to please others:

> No, let the candied tongue lick absurd pomp,
> And crook the pregnant hinges of the knee
> Where thrift may follow fawning. Dost thou hear?
> Since my dear soul was mistress of her choice,
> And could of men distinguish her election,
> Sh'ath seal'd thee for herself; for thou hast been
> As one, in suff'ring all, that suffers nothing. (III.ii.60–66)

He goes on to talk of fortune; Horatio is constant over time and change of fortune. As we would say, he has integrity, or wholeness, consistency of character. Again we see Hamlet probing and defining, revealing hidden truths in himself and others. As we approach the play within the play, we begin to appreciate the subtlety and coherence of his philosophy. He will "interpret" the action of the dumb show for Ophelia, just as maliciously he contends he could interpret the action between her and her lover (III.ii.240–41). Hamlet as philosopher is then to the world what Hamlet as dramatic critic is to the play: he reads beneath the action to the hidden significance.

When Claudius storms from the chamber having seen his crime revealed in the play, Rosencrantz and Guildenstern are set on Hamlet again, and he abuses them for attempting to play upon him as a pipe: "you would pluck out the heart of my mystery" (356). Polonius then attempts to hurry him along to his mother's chamber, but there is opportunity for Hamlet to force the old man into seeing in the clouds anything Hamlet pretends to see:

Hamlet: Do you see yonder cloud that's almost in shape of a camel?
Polonius: By th' mass and 'tis—like a camel indeed.
Hamlet: Methinks it is like a weasel.
Polonius: It is backed like a weasel.
Hamlet: Or like a whale.
Polonius: Very like a whale.
Hamlet: Then I will come to my mother by and by. (366–74)

Again, Shakespeare misses no opportunity for calling our attention to Hamlet's perception and the failure of others to keep up with him. So far superior is he to them in both intellectual insight and creativity that he sometimes seems to be writing his own play. Like a puppet master, he pulls their strings.

In the short soliloquy that ends the scene, Hamlet takes on another role, or rather the very role he has refused so far: the conventional hero of revenge:

> 'Tis now the very witching time of night,
> When churchyards yawn and hell itself breathes out
> Contagion to this world. Now could I drink hot blood,
> And do such bitter business as the day
> Would quake to look on. (379–83)

Here only we the audience overhear him, but, anachronistically, we have the image of his twirling his mustaches in a silent film melodrama: it is a caricature of a type well known in his own day, and we cannot imagine him speaking these lines without self-irony.

What happens next is truly extraordinary: Claudius, the villain, is given a soliloquy. He is at prayer, but realizes he cannot save his soul as long as he keeps the prizes of his sin: crown and queen. This is not the first time Claudius has been allowed such a moment; earlier, just before Claudius and Polonius position themselves for Hamlet's "To be, or not to be," Claudius observes, aside, in reference to Polonius's image of the devil sugared over with piety:

> . . . O 'tis too true.
> How smart a lash that speech doth give my conscience.
> The harlot's cheek, beautied with plast'ring art,

> Is not more ugly to the thing that helps it
> Than is my deed to my most painted word. (III.i.48–54)

Women wearing makeup to conceal their blemishes is consistently used as a metaphor for hypocrisy and self-blindness; we find it also in the nunnery scene immediately following (III.i.144–51) and in the graveyard scene (V.i.186–89). Surely Shakespeare allows Claudius opportunities to bear his soul so that we can appreciate the more Hamlet's perception of his guilt.

Hamlet delivers a brief soliloquy here, arguing with himself about the nature of revenge: if he kills Claudius at prayer, does he not run the risk of sending his soul straight to heaven? This kind of consideration is conventional in the revenge tragedy. We should also recall the Ghost's insistence that Claudius had killed his brother:

> Cut off even in the blossoms of my sin,
> Unhousel'd, disappointed, unanel'd,
> No reck'ning made, but sent to my account
> With all my imperfections on my head. (I.v.76–79)

Thus his soul is now in purgatory. Also, in the first meeting with Horatio, Hamlet had used the expression, in reference to his mother's marriage to Claudius, "Would I had met my dearest foe in heaven / Or ever I had seen that day, Horatio" (I.ii.182–83). Such considerations seem to us academic and absurd; it is difficult here to determine what effect Shakespeare intended, and indeed had on his original audience. Presumably even they would have taken this refusal to act as both conventional and peculiarly appropriate to Hamlet's character as so far developed: he has ratified the ghost's account of Claudius's guilt with the ruse of the play within the play; now, almost in answer to his earlier prayer that his thoughts be bloody, he finds the villain unattended, a sacrificial victim at the altar. And yet he does not kill him.

Another turn of contradiction takes place in his mother's chamber; though he has told himself to sheathe his sword (III.iii.88), he bursts in upon her with it drawn. (Cf. Oedipus's entering Iocasta's chamber with his sword drawn in Sophocles' play; he has the intention there to kill her, whereas Hamlet has warned himself not to follow the example of Nero, who killed his mother [III.ii.386–90].) This, together with his riddling responses to her questions, cause her alarm. When she cries out, "Thou wilt not murder me? Help, ho!" (III.iv.20), Polonius, behind the arras, echoes her: "What ho! Help!" Hamlet then thrusts his sword through the arras and kills the old man. When Polonius collapses dead and Gertrude cries out again, Hamlet asks, "Is it the King?" (26). How can he think this when he has just left Claudius at prayer? He would have no reason to think anyone else to be in his mother's chamber, and in delaying his revenge in the previous scene, he fantasized the opportunity of killing Claudius "In th' incestuous pleasure of his bed" (III.iii.90). We have seen earlier, and will soon be reminded, that Hamlet is obsessed with the scene of Gertrude and Claudius's lovemaking. Thus Hamlet's actual "madness" overrules his reason here, and momentarily he imagines himself having fulfilled his desire for appropriate vengeance. When he realizes he has killed the old man, he is barely interrupted in his intention to "speak daggers" to his mother:

Queen: O what a rash and bloody deed is this!

Hamlet: A bloody deed. Almost as bad, good mother,
           As kill a king and marry with his brother. (III.iv.26–28)

Again Hamlet draws the contrast between the two brothers:

> Look here upon this picture, and on this,
> The counterfeit presentment of two brothers.
> See what a grace was seated on this brow,
> Hyperion's curls, the front of Jove himself, . . .
> This was your husband. Look you now what follows.
> Here is your husband, like a mildew'd ear
> Blasting his wholesome brother. (III.iv.53–65)

Again the emphasis is on the contrast: these two brothers are as unlike each other as is possible, and yet Gertrude seems to have confused them, to have taken the one for the other. (This will be the issue in Shakespeare's later play *The Winter's Tale*.). The abuse Hamlet heaps on his mother here is a recapitulation of what he has said about her in his first soliloquy ("Frailty, thy name is woman") and then against Ophelia in the nunnery scene. In the thematic structure of the play, as well as in its plot, this scene marks a climax: vengeance against the murderer of his father is displaced against its cause, the faithless woman, just as the vengeance itself is displaced from its primary target against the meddling old courtier. This does not satisfy the Ghost, who appears here to Hamlet—and to him alone—to "whet [his] almost blunted purpose" (111). He feels pity for Gertrude, who, he reminds his son, is weak in flesh and therefore vulnerable to "conceit" (i.e., imagination). Hamlet's deflection of his vengeance and vituperation from the male to the female—against the Ghost's instructions, who insisted in his first appearance, "Leave her to heaven" (I.v.86)—should be related to other aspects of his character. Just as in the nunnery scene, where Hamlet warned Ophelia, "Wise men know well enough what monsters you [women] make of them," and "I have heard of your paintings well enough" (140–44), so here he sees his duty as that of discovery and exposure: "You go not till I set up a glass / Where you may see the inmost part of you" (18–19). Truth is hidden, and his mission is to expose it. The soliloquies, as we have seen, expose himself to himself; now these dialogue scenes expose others to themselves.

The first three scenes of Act IV are short, devoted to discovering Polonius's body and dispatching Hamlet to England. Then comes the last of the great soliloquies, "How all occasions do inform against me" (IV.iv.32–66). This speech is found only in Q2. It has been taken as the *catastasis*—that moment in the forward action of the drama when everything comes to a halt and the hero considers the significance of it all. It essentially repeats the self-analysis we heard from Hamlet in the second soliloquy, "O what a rogue and peasant slave am I" (II.ii.544–601), when he determined on a course of action. The difference here is that there is comparison of his case with Fortinbras's, which takes us back to the similarities between them suggested in Act I, scenes 1 and 2: Fortinbras is out in the world avenging his father's death at the hands of Hamlet's father. Here, though, Hamlet questions the wisdom of the young prince who would sacrifice the lives of twenty thousand men for a piece of land not large enough to bury them in. He nevertheless ends his meditation with the injunction, "O from this time forth / My thoughts be bloody or be nothing worth."

The rest of Act IV is devoted to the madness and suicide of Ophelia and the plotting of Hamlet's murder by Claudius and Laertes: here Laertes, as previously Fortinbras, is held up as an antitype to Hamlet. Laertes' father has been killed, and Laertes will stop at nothing to avenge him. Again, the comparison seems negative: Laertes supplements Claudius's treachery—the point of Laertes' foil in the fencing match will not be protected—with his own: he will anoint that same foil with poison so Hamlet will surely die, even of the slightest wound. The whole idea of a duel is to determine the difference between the two combatants: who is the better swordsman? Throughout the scene where it is planned (IV.vii) and then again when its terms are presented to Hamlet by Osric (V.ii), there is emphasis on the degrees of difference within the category of gentleman or courtier. Hamlet maintains throughout the play, and especially at its close, that each man is unique and can be judged only by his own standards, against himself.

The point of the graveyard scene is both to relieve the tension before the catastrophe and to show that Hamlet is no longer concerned with the threat of damnation in an afterlife: he faces Yorick's skull and says, essentially, "This is all there is; there is no other life; there is death and then nothing." This is presented as a new way of seeing the human condition, at which he has arrived after his escape from death on the voyage to England. In a series of remarks to Horatio immediately before the duel, he expresses his acceptance of a force operating in nature that is beyond the control of man, and his comprehension:

> There's a divinity that shapes our ends,
> Rough-hew them how we will— (V.ii.10–11)

Some have seen here the invocation of a Christian, specifically Protestant, notion of divine providence; Hamlet even uses the word "providence" in his reference to the biblical passage about the fall of a sparrow (215–20).

It is crucial to our understanding of Shakespeare's whole notion of tragedy whether we accept this argument: if Hamlet yields himself up to fate or into the hands of God, then he does the opposite of what the heroes of Greek tragedy do. Oedipus, Ajax, and Antigone all seize the moment when they seem most limited in their choices and make that moment their own, even if it means suicide or self-blinding: "The gods made me do it, but the deed was mine." Another strain of recent criticism argues the opposite for late Elizabethan–early Jacobean tragedy, though not specifically for *Hamlet*: rather than show the tragic hero caught up in circumstances beyond his control and suffering with the guilty although he is himself less guilty, this different type of tragedy points up the contradiction between man's expectation of order in the world and what the hero actually experiences (Dollimore). We need only see that the structure of the play—the way the action moves forward with the development of theme and character—draws attention to its own discontinuities and redirections. It is not a well-made play; we have certain expectations, and these are not satisfied in proper sequence, but rather delayed and deflected. Rather than accuse Shakespeare of ineptitude, it seems better to consider that these irregularities are part of his plan. Just as the soliloquies call attention to the contrast between the seen and the unseen, so the discontinuities call attention to the contrast beween intention and accomplishment.

LANGUAGE AND IMAGERY

Like everything else in the play, the language of *Hamlet* is varied and complex; indeed Hamlet himself speaks in several distinct styles. The basic style is elevated and elaborate, the language of the court. Castiglione advises courtiers to strive for novelty in their speech, to collect witty expressions and revise them so as to delight their prince with the freshness of their invention. But within courtly diction itself, there are several variations. Claudius speaks in balanced phrases, developing his long sentences in what is called "periodic" style, incorporating many rhetorical figures (anaphora, hendiadys, paronomasia, etc.). Then Polonius speaks in his own distinctively self-conscious version of courtly diction, calling attention to his own cleverness, and often, as Gertrude complains, allowing "art" to distort and delay "matter." Finally, there is Osric, who strains so to describe familiar objects and exercises in an unfamiliar manner that he seems absurd. Indeed, Hamlet offers a parody of Osric which is a *reductio ad absurdum* of courtly diction. As we shall see, other characters also speak in highly rhetorical styles, sometimes unexpectedly—for example, Ophelia, at the end of the nunnery scene, when one would expect her to be distraught and therefore disorderly in her speech, delivers a textbook example of a character sketch of Hamlet. Then, of course, there is the more straightforward diction of Horatio, Marcellus, and other attendants, and finally the language of the "Clowns," the gravediggers in Act V. There is thus a social hierarchy of speech, but also the more subtle characterization by speech: Polonius is the garrulous old man, Claudius the new ruler trying to sound regal. All of this happens in other of Shakespeare's plays. What sets *Hamlet* apart is the variety within the speech of the main character; here Shakespeare seems determined to show us a character of such infinite variety that he speaks many different languages.

Cantor calls our attention to some rhetorical features of Claudius's opening speech and interprets these as characterizing devices (77–78). For instance, note how consistent he is in his use of the "royal first-person plural":

> Though yet of Hamlet our dear brother's death
> The memory be green, and that it us befitted
> To bear our hearts in grief and our whole kingdom
> To be contracted in one brow of woe,
> Yet so far hath discretion fought with nature
> That we with wisest sorrow think on him
> Together with remembrance of ourselves. (I.ii.1–7)

Cantor warns us of Shakespeare's subtle intentions: "Given our knowledge of Claudius' duplicity, we might wish to detect a false note in his speech, but in fact part of Shakespeare's initial effort to show Claudius in command as king is to show him in command of the language of a king" (78). He goes on to compare such "legitimate monarchs" as Henry V and Lear.

Within these seven lines we can distinguish a number of figures common in courtly diction. The repertoire of such figures derives ultimately from the theory and practice of Greek political and litigious speechwriting. The concerns were for a pleasing and arresting play of sound and sense. For instance, we notice at the beginning of lines 3 and 4 the repetition of sounds: "To bear . . . / To be . . ." The name given this figure is *anaphora*, or "carrying over." There are two striking metaphors, examples of catachresis: "The memory be green," and "our whole kingdom / . . . contracted in one brow of woe." The first treats the human capacity to remember as if it were a plant, and the second personifies the kingdom so that it can have one brow. (The first metaphor will fit into one of the most prominent patterns of imagery throughout the play, of gardens and trees.) Again personification is used in "discretion fought with nature." Finally the order of the words and phrases in the last two lines speaks precisely of Claudius's concern: usurpation. Note how "we" stands close to the beginning of the first line and "ourselves" at the end of the second; within this frame stands "him."

Hamlet shows in his response—Claudius and his mother request him to stay at court and not return to Wittenberg—that he is in complete control of the rhetorical art. Gertrude has asked of his grief, "Why seems it so particular with thee?"

> Seems, madam? Nay, it is. I know not "seems."
> 'Tis not alone my inky cloak, good mother,
> Nor customary suits of solemn black,
> Nor windy suspiration of forc'd breath,
> No, nor the fruitful river in the eye,
> Nor the dejected haviour of the visage,
> Together with all forms, moods, shapes of grief,
> That can denote me truly. These indeed seem,
> For they are actions that a man might play;
> But I have that within which passes show,
> These but the trappings and the suits of woe. (I.ii.76–86)

Like Claudius—perhaps even to better him rhetorically—Hamlet employs anaphora stretching over four lines: "Nor . . . / Nor . . . / No . . . / Nor." Also personification and catachresis are evident: tears are the "river of the eye," and it is, like a tree, "fruitful." He adds asyndeton, the joining of a series without conjunctions: "forms, moods, shapes." Finally there is a developed metaphor in the last three lines: "actions a man might play / . . . show / . . . trappings." Hamlet compares his grief to a play acted out on stage in costume; this introduces one of the most consistent allusions in the play, which is to the relation between theatre and reality. It precisely explains Hamlet's philosophical and psychological point, the difference between illusion ("seems") and reality. I should think on stage that the actor playing Claudius would step backward at this point, in admiration at the younger man's rhetorical expertise. We compare Hamlet's concision with Claudius's expansiveness. Indeed this whole scene is drawn up like an agon, a contest, between Claudius and Hamlet: they are enemies, antagonists, in competition for the throne and the love of Gertrude, and Shakespeare first presents them to us in a rhetorical agon with the audience of the court, wherein they display their skills of both reason and expression.

In Hamlet's last line, he uses a figure that several critics have remarked as the dominant rhetorical figure in the play: hendiadys, which is saying one thing through two words. There is only a slight difference between "trappings" and "suits," in their reference to the costumes of mourning. The actor delivering the line might pause between them, making "suits" an afterthought, an attempt to define his meaning more closely, or to emphasize it by repetition. Claudius will soon use hendiadys in his commendation of Hamlet's yielding to Gertrude's entreaty that he stay: "Why, 'tis a loving and a fair reply" (121). "Loving" and "fair" are not synonyms, but put together in this way they create the image of perfect filial behavior. He has said, "I shall in all my best obey you, madam" (120), which shows his love for her and is fairly, that is, beautifully, expressed. Wright has argued that the introduction of the article "a" in Claudius's hendiadys slightly "estranges" the two components. He compares *Othello* (V.ii.313): "a malignant and a turbaned Turk." He goes on to offer other fine distinctions in Shakespeare's use of the figure. In particular he cites Laertes' phrase, used to warn Ophelia, "shot and danger of desire," as peculiarly Virgilian, in that one of the elements is concrete and the other abstract: "shot" is an actual blast of firearms, but "danger" is atmosphere or circumstance.

Virgil's use is very subtle: it allows him in the *Aeneid* to speak simultaneously on the level of narrative and philosophically. Virgil is ultimately the source of the First Player's speech on the fall of Troy (II.ii.445ff.); in Book II of the *Aeneid* the hero recounts to Dido that disaster. In the course of the speech, which contains many fine rhetorical devices, there is a wonderful example of "transferred epithet": "Pyrrhus' bleeding sword" (487): a sword causes wounds to bleed, but can be said to bleed itself only metaphorically. Charney (5) distinguishes this and other features of the speech as peculiarly "Marlovian," that is, suggesting the style of Christopher Marlowe. Thus certain figures become associated with certain authors. Indeed, so characteristic is rhetorical usage that statistics can sometimes help determine authorship: Donald Foster has analyzed "The Funeral Elegy for Mr. William Peters" rhetorically and with the aid of the computer compared other Elizabethan texts, and found that the style fits Shakespeare best of all Elizabethan poets, and peculiarly the style of Shakespeare toward the end of his career.

The greatest concentration of hendiadys comes in Ophelia's speech at the end of the nunnery scene:

> O, what a noble mind is here o'erthrown!
> The courtier's, soldier's, scholar's, eye, tongue, sword,
> Th' expectancy and rose of the fair state,
> The glass of fashion and the mould of form,
> Th' observ'd of all observers, quite, quite down!

And I, of ladies most deject and wretched,
That suck'd the honey of his music vows,
Now see that noble and most sovereign reason
Like sweet bells jangled out of tune and harsh,
That unmatch'd form and feature of blown youth
Blasted with ecstasy. O woe is me
T' have seen what I have seen, see what I see. (III.i.152–63)

There are six examples of hendiadys in eleven lines; there are other figures here as well, such as asyndeton, paronomasia, and catachresis. Heightened emotion can, of course, find finest expression in highly rhetorical language, but here it seems out of character. I am reminded of some of Juliet's speeches, for instance, where she responds to her mother's tirade against Romeo for having killed Tybalt with consistent ambiguity: "Would none that I might venge my cousin's death" (III.v.87). It is considered characteristic of Shakespeare early in his career to indulge in such rhetorical cleverness even though it might not suit the dramatic situation or the character. But what of *Hamlet*, written at the height of his mature powers? Did he become obsessed with hendiadys and simply fall into its attractive possibilities at seemingly inappropriate moments? Wright has argued instead that hendiadys fits with a deeper preoccupation in the play, and that is its doubling and pairing and comparing—what he calls the "dual phenomenon" (80). Bernardo calls Horatio and Marcellus "the rivals of my watch" (I.i.14). Then there are the pairs of Cornelius and Voltemand, Rosencrantz and Guildenstern. The ghost is consistently described as "like" the dead king. Thematically, Hamlet is compared with Fortinbras and Laertes and provided with a friend, Horatio, whom Hamlet considers his own external soul. This should convince us, at least in Shakespeare, to take rhetorical figures seriously. They are not just decoration but rather the revelation of the poet's deepest intentions. We are not what we seem to be; we are not the roles we play. We have within us a hidden core of being that is consistent over time and, moreover, what we are is unique to ourselves; we are not duplicated in the world here and now, but only in that image of ourselves that we ourselves formulate and project to others.

Charney (258–313) distinguishes in Hamlet's own speeches four different styles: self-conscious, witty, passionate, and simple. He also recognizes that Hamlet has a critical attitude toward language; here a major theme, characterization, and imagery all come together, since it is Hamlet's obsession with how one presents oneself in speech—as in the theatre—as opposed to how one thinks of oneself in private, that defines one philosophically. Indeed, Charney calls attention to parody as the crucial aspect of Hamlet's "self-conscious style." This is most notable in his baiting of Osric:

Osric: Sir, here is newly come to court Laertes—believe me, an absolute gentleman, full of most excellent differences, of very soft society and great showing. Indeed, to speak feelingly of him, he is the card or calendar of gentry;
for you shall find in him the continent of what part a gentleman would see.

Hamlet: Sir, his definement suffers no perdition in you, though I know to divide him
inventorially would dozy th' arithmetic of memory, and yet but yaw neither,
in respect of his quick sail. But, in the verity of extolment; I take him to be a
soul of great article and his infusion of such dearth and rareness as, to make
true diction of him, his semblable is his mirror and who else would trace him
his umbrage, nothing more.

Osric: Your lordship speaks most infallibly of him. (V.ii.105–21)

Osric does not even know that he is being ridiculed: Hamlet can so perfectly capture, duplicate, and surpass each of Osric's foolish figures—neologisms, hyperbole, catachresis—that he arouses in him admiration rather than
consternation. This mastery of other characters' language—and Charney
points out that Hamlet can also catch the style of Laertes and Claudius—puts
Hamlet above the action of the play and makes of him, with Shakespeare,
coauthor. In correcting their style, he also corrects their philosophy. We note
that Osric claims Laertes is the best example of chivalry, the defining member
of a class. Hamlet corrects this, insisting that Laertes is unique—that all others can try to do is imitate him.

Hamlet's witty style depends on puns. This again is a vehicle for ridicule—
he uses it particularly on Polonius—and since he is passing for mad, he is
given license. We recall that Amleth in Saxo, though seeming to speak nonsense, always precisely speaks the truth. When Polonius observes of Hamlet,
"Though this be madness, yet there is method in 't" (II.ii.205), and further,
"How pregnant sometimes his replies are—a happiness that often madness
hits on, which reason and sanity could not so prosperously be delivered of"
(208–11), he suggests the modern, essentially Freudian perception that punning is compulsive with schizophrenics: their break from reality gives them a
different orientation in language; they manipulate it. The world is not real to
them, so they do not pursue the naive notion that language reflects reality. By
changing the meaning of words, they can change things. Hamlet's most "pregnant" punning is found in the scene of the play within the play:

Hamlet: Lady, shall I lie in your lap?

Ophelia: No, my lord.

Hamlet: I mean, my head upon your lap.

Ophelia: Ay, my lord.

Hamlet: Do you think I meant country matters?

Ophelia: I think nothing, my lord.

Hamlet: That's a fair thought to lie between maids' legs.

Ophelia: What is, my lord?

Hamlet: Nothing. (III.ii.110–19)

The puns begin with "lie," which carries both the innocent and the sexual meaning: "to lie in love with." When Hamlet sees that Ophelia has taken the latter, he continues with a pun on "country," referring to bawdy, rustic behavior, but the first syllable also specifies the female genitalia. Ophelia characteristically refuses to admit that she had thought any such thing, but Hamlet takes her "nothing" in two senses: "it is a fair thought to lie with a woman in love," and "what lies between a woman's legs is a fair thing to think of." When Ophelia again fails to keep up, Hamlet has to explain, with the final pun: "a woman's thing is nothing." This is a daunting display of wit, but it does not stand in isolation from larger concerns of theme and character. Ophelia in her madness will compulsively sing bawdy songs; her father's death lifts that repression of her sexual nature that he and her brother had both imposed. Laertes will at that point observe of Ophelia's speech, "This nothing's more than matter" (IV.v.172). Madness and sexuality are then brought into conjunction in a way that gives meaning to Polonius's interpretation of Hamlet's madness: "Still harping on my daughter" (II.ii.187). Hamlet feigns madness (but also shows signs of true madness) after his father's death and his mother's overhasty remarriage; Ophelia actually does go mad after her father's death at the hands of Hamlet. For both, madness is a kind of freedom—a license to speak truth. Those who hear them listen carefully, expecting to find something of substance in their speech. Is it they, the audience, who make something out of nothing, or is it the mad who make something out of the nothing of ordinary experience? Beyond the obvious joke on a woman's thing being nothing—she does not have the man's thing—there is the joking reference to the mystery of conception, pregnancy, and birth: out of that nothing comes something. Hamlet warns Polonius of the dangers of conception, suggesting it can take place spontaneously in the sunlight (II.ii.181–85). We are left with the impression that Hamlet's verbal brillance is like life itself: it creates out of what seems not to exist, or, as Theseus in *A Midsummer Night's Dream* says of the imagination of "the lunatic, the lover and the poet," it "gives to airy nothing a local habitation and a name" (V.i.16–17).

Charney's category of "passionate style" is essentially that of the soliloquies; here he argues against the critics who see in these speeches Shakespeare's own primary concerns, his most serious attempts to express his own worldview, and shows that they are rather characterized by rapid changes in direction, thus capturing Hamlet's disordered but always fruitful imagination. Besides the frequent use of ellipsis, interjection, hyperbaton, and other figures that interrupt logical development, they are marked by metaphors that spring spontaneously from the subject matter, with none of the feel of belabored or artificial conception we find in more contrived passages. The first soliloquy is an index to all that follow:

> O that this too, too sullied flesh would melt,
> Thaw and resolve itself into a dew,
> Or that the Everlasting had not fix'd
> His canon 'gainst self-slaughter. O God! God!
> How weary, stale, flat and unprofitable
> Seem to me all the uses of this world!
> Fie on 't, ah fie. 'tis an unweeded garden
> That grows to seed; things rank and gross in nature
> Possess it merely. That it should come to this!
> But two months dead—nay, not so much, not two—
> So excellent a king, that was to this
> Hyperion to a satyr, so loving to my mother
> That he might not beteem the winds of heaven
> Visit her face too roughly. Heaven and earth,
> Must I remember? Why, she would hang on him
> As if increase of appetite had grown
> By what it fed on; and yet within a month—
> Let me not think on 't—Frailty, thy name is woman—
> A little month, or ere those shoes were old
> With which she follow'd my poor father's body,
> Like Niobe, all tears—why, she—
> O God, a beast that wants discourse of reason
> Would have mourn'd longer—married with my uncle,
> My father's brother—but no more like my father
> Than I to Hercules. Within a month,
> Ere yet the salt of most unrighteous tears
> Had left the flushing in her galled eyes,
> She married—O most wicked speed! To post
> With such dexterity to incestuous sheets!
> It is not, nor it cannot come to good. (I.ii.129–58)

In this twenty-nine-line speech, there are very few complete sentences. The speaker keeps interrupting himself to express disgust or add detail. It seems the thought is not linear and therefore will not yield to ordinary development, but rather is a cluster of associations around which the speaker circles, jabbing at the center of his concern. His thought and expression are truly an organic whole. Having seen Gertrude and Claudius hold court together in the earlier part of the scene and heard Claudius describe her as "th' imperial jointress," Hamlet has a vivid picture in his mind of their actual copulation; hence the climax of his meditation is their "incestuous sheets." But from the first, other disgusting images intrude upon him, primarily that of "an unweeded garden": the ungovernable sexuality of his mother manifests itself to him as something "rank and gross in nature." Further, her sexual desire is an appetite that can never know satiety but grows greater the more it is fed. These are ideas that will find similar expression in the nunnery and the closet scenes. At base there is a virulent misogyny: the woman is seen as too weak rationally—"Frailty, thy name is woman!"—to control her bestial instincts. Since this disgust with women begins with his mother, a mature woman, and is then transferred to the virginal, young Ophelia, we might follow the Freudian critics who see in the garden imagery of the play an obsession with female pubic hair. If we can judge by Hamlet's "pretraumatic" Petrarchan sonnet to Ophelia—"*To the celestial and my soul's idol, the most beautified Ophelia, these; in her excellent white bosom, these . . .*"—he had thought of her as perfect, like a statue, without human marks or qualities. When his mother shows herself sexually incontinent, his abhorrence will extend to all women. He is still harping on their deceit—"paint an inch thick"—in the graveyard scene.

In reading the soliloquies, it is helpful to recall a German term for the device: *Selbstgesprach*, "self-address." The point is not just that the character is alone on stage—*solus, loquor*—but that he talks to himself as if he were in dialogue with another character. The term "internal monologue" is also helpful. W. Clemens offers this observation: the soliloqies represent a "new kind of dramatic speech which by its rapid transitions, its dissolution of syntax, its extraordinary economy and its fusion of several emotions and ideas can follow the quickly changing reactions of a sensitive mind better than speech in dialogue ever could" (quoted by Charney, 304). It is thought in the process of formation, and it is thought that springs forth spontaneously from the main character without the prodding of a protactic character—one who has no function other than to ask the protagonist what he is thinking. The soliloquy then not only provides the character with a release for his emotions but also a framework for his thinking about himself.

To talk to oneself in this manner proves there is a self to talk to. These speeches of Hamlet are deliberative, allowing him to realize things about himself he had never dared consider. They are thus quite different from the monologues of the Senecan tradition, which are both rhetorically more studied and psychologically less profound. Senecan heroes tend only to boast in their monologues, or wonder what horror they can commit that is worse than all that has already been done.

Charney's final category for Hamlet's speeches is the simple style. Here he is concerned primarily with those narrative bits and pieces wherein Hamlet shows he can describe things straightforwardly:

> I had my father's signet in my purse,
> Which was the model of that Danish seal,
> Folded the writ up in the form of th' other,
> Subscrib'd it, gave 't th' impression, plac'd it safely,
> The changeling never known. (V.ii.49–53)

But the last words Hamlet speaks to Horatio before their entry into the fencing arena at the end of the play is in this same simple style:

We defy augury. There is special providence in the fall of a sparrow. If it be now, 'tis not to come; if it be not to come, it will be now; if it be not now, yet it will come. The readiness is all. Since no man, of aught he leaves, knows aught, what is 't to leave betimes. (V.ii.215–20)

Most obviously this precisely answers his two soliloquies on suicide, "Would that this too too sullied flesh would melt" (I.ii.129–58) and "To be, or not to be" (II.i.56–88), but stylistically it is an answer too. In the previous speeches, Hamlet's mind is open to all sorts of ideas and images, propositions and opportunities; here, when he has finally decided on a course of action, his statement is almost mathematically concise.

4

THEMES

In this survey of approaches to and opinion of *Hamlet*, certain themes have been repeated in various forms. The most consistent pattern is contrast: Hamlet contrasted with Fortinbras and Laertes, true friendship with fawning hypocrisy, the spiritual with the physical, the changing with the unchanging, art with nature. In the bewildering variety of the play these stand out as the figure in the carpet. Hamlet seeks to fly from the world of inconsistency and illusion to a realm of constant truth. Paradoxically, his efforts lead him to imitate those he most despises: he makes up plays and would himself be an actor (*hypokrites*), and on the voyage to England he pulls a trick on Rosencrantz and Guildenstern that would credit the most Machiavellian courtier.

With his return to court, the crucial question is: To what extent does he will the action that leads finally to his revenge and death? Here we should recall Hegel's description of "the beautiful soul," the romantic hero who condemns the world and withdraws from it, not realizing that he himself is a product of it and carries its form impressed on him (*Phenomenology* VI.C.c). Does Hamlet ever come to see himself in this light? To Ophelia in the nunnery scene he describes himself as "proud, revengeful, ambitious, with more offences," and in his last exchanges with Horatio before the duel, there is a calm acceptance of the currents of life that lead to death or fulfillment: "A man's life's but to say 'one,'" and, "There is a special providence in the fall of a sparrow." Hamlet, accepting the terms and conditions of the duel, marks a reversal in both attitude and practice: he enters into the rituals of the court whereas he had previously ridiculed them ("a custom more honored in the breach than the observance") and whereas he had before always seen through its various charades to the hidden meaning beneath, now he allows himself to be fatally fooled.

Some critics take this as indication that Shakespeare contrasts older feudal, and Catholic, attitudes toward human responsibility with more recent Protestant teaching on the power of divine providence. Some have even claimed that Hamlet's acquiescence in the forces of intrigue makes him less than tragic: we prefer our heroes to die with "harness on," fully aware of the confrontation between their indomitable spirit and the unyielding forces of circumstance. Still others recognize that the tragic hero is defined not by his difference in kind from the world but his difference in quality: he is better than other men, but not essentially different. To accept this as his lot in life — "O cursed spite that I was ever born to set it right"—is the great recognition; for the hero who is primarily intellectual rather than active, knowing is more important than doing. He might botch his revenge, but he sees himself clearly at the end and wants his story to be told aright.

One way of construing this development is that Hamlet has finally relinquished his idealism—his attempt to live his life separate and apart from other mere mortals. He has now entered the fray and proved himself mortal. This contradiction of his almost Christlike pretensions need not be seen as defeat. With it comes another large and important concession. In Olivier's film, Gertrude drinks the poisoned cup knowingly, in order to save her son. Hamlet might have some sense of this when he says, "Wretched Queen, adieu." This justly concludes Olivier's overall Freudian reading of the play: Hamlet's obsession with his mother has led to his disaster. He had insisted she remain virginal and pure, assimilating her to the lady of the courtly love tradition, refusing to allow that a woman might have sexual desires. Now he accepts her frailty: flesh is heir to desire as well as death.

These two developments are not unrelated. Throughout, the most characteristic features of Hamlet's mind are his metaphysics and his misogyny. We see them as, respectively, the crucial philosophical and psychological tenets of the play. Clearly Hamlet gives up his metaphysics in the graveyard: holding the skull of Yorick, he realizes that this is all there is, that there is no life after death and therefore no need to fear eternal damnation. There is only the here and now, and all that matters is how we perform in it. At that point he is still railing on the falseness of women: "Now get you to my lady's chamber and tell her, let her paint an inch thick, to this favor she most come." Then he sees Ophelia dead, though it must be admitted that this does not seem to move him as much as the adversarial grief of Laertes. His last exchange with her had been on "Nothing," that bawdy word play by which he confused the woman's private parts with the philosophical speculation, "Nothing can come of nothing." If we can allow that Hamlet is reconciled with his mother before he dies and that he has renounced his expectations of any world beyond this, then in both cases he has made something of nothing. Indeed he himself is that something, since he was born of his mother's body, and in accepting his mortality he aligns himself with her as a creature of the flesh. Like the blind Oedipus then—who struck out his eyes with the pins from his wife-mother's dress so he would never have to look on her body again—he sees and knows before he dies. This is tragedy of the highest order, and so *Hamlet* repays the great effort we make in reading and rereading, viewing and reviewing, and thinking on it over and over again.

In subsequent readings and viewings, we become more deeply aware of what may be Shakespeare's most characteristic theme: the mutuality of art and life. We begin to entertain the proposition that Shakespeare in his particular genius, but composing at his particular moment in the evolution of Western intellectual history, may have fulfilled what was only a potential for tragedy when Aeschylus, Sophocles, and Euripides defined the genre two millennia before him. Tragedy, which was originally only Athenian and peculiarly fifth century, was always concerned with the relation between seeing and being and knowing: it is not for nothing that the greatest of the Greek tragic heroes is Oedipus, who had to blind himself to see, because he does not know who he is while he has sight in his eyes. This negation, which yields a previously un-revealed positive, is highly suggestive. It makes us think of Lacan's definition of masculinity: it is known only under the threat of castration. Eyes and testicles are not only the same shape but are referred to by the same word in Greek: *kykloi*, "circles." Freud enlightened us on the mental functioning of displacement upward, but only after Hegel made *Aufhebung* the principle of his whole philosophy. How is it that something that is "canceled out" becomes something more important later? What is sublimation, and how does it characterize the tragic hero generally, the Shakespearean tragic hero more particularly, and Hamlet most of all?

"Metatheatre" is a term coined analogically with Aristotle's "metaphysics" to denote that turn of mind common to Shakespeare, Velásquez, Cervantes, and other great artists of the early seventeenth century (e.g., Abel, but see Calderwood 200, n. 26, for other references). Foucault has said very precise things about the continental exponents of this international movement, but he was relatively innocent of Shakespeare. He said, of Velásquez and Cervantes—and all the lesser French lights whom he knew well—that they gave up on the Aristotelian proposition that art imitates life and decided instead that art is an imitation of imitation: it describes and defines the artistic process. This is a form of negation—or rather a comment on the nothing that might be there but which art turns into something. If art can only define the artistic process, then what is its subject, and wherein does its truth lie?

Very boldly put, I think *Hamlet* is about nothing. I think this is what Hamlet sees in nature. It will surprise no one who knows *Lear* that the relation between nature and nothing is a Shakespearean theme. Lear warns Cordelia, "Nothing will come of nothing" (I.i.89). Later he instructs Regan:

> O, reason not the need! Out basest beggars
> Are in the poorest thing superfluous.
> Allow not nature more than nature needs,
> Man's life is cheap as beast's. (II.iv.204–7)

Then he goes on the heath, strips himself naked, and goes mad. Human nature reduced to nothing is nothing. There is nothing essentially there in nature to support man in his pretensions to be more than bestial. It is all a matter of his invention, of his creative urge to fill the gap he perceives.

In *Hamlet* the gap is in the woman's body—Ophelia's "nothing"—and in Hamlet's metaphysical pretensions: he would make of himself something god-like; he would be pure spirit, like his father; he would negate his flesh. This is where Shakespeare's particular place in intellectual history provides him with perhaps the supreme tragic statement, the fulfillment of what was only potential in Greek tragedy. In the Western tradition, between the Greek tragedies and Shakespeare, come successively Plato, who hypostatized a world of perfect and unchanging Forms, removed from and only barely distinguishable in the world of sensual experience; then the Neoplatonic Christian church fathers, who put God in the place of Plato's Forms; and then the courtly love tradition, which put the lady in place of God. When Shakespeare forces Hamlet to face the nothing of his existence—as flesh of his mother's flesh and as uncertainty in his search for absolute truth—he announces the end of the courtly love tradition and one major movement in the history of metaphysics.

What survives is another major tenet of Renaissance humanism: man as artist imitates God as creator of the world. Out of the seemingly exhaustive pessimism of seeing the world as nothing springs the infinite possibility of man's creative spirit—and this is Hamlet's essential character, Shakespeare's essential theme. We then see the play as a paring away of all of man's fallacious expectations—the reduction of his pretensions—to nothing, as in Lear on the heath. And yet simultaneously we see Hamlet as sonneteer, playwright, philosopher and, finally, in the burden he passes on to Horatio, autobiographer. He has made himself up out of nothing, and that is his tragic achievement. The world is nothing, and he has been reduced to nothing, but in seeing this and accepting it—though at the same time recasting it in his own perfect image of himself—he has redeemed that nothing and made of himself something we cannot not acknowledge to be. Christlike he transfigures himself. This was a model unavailable to the Greeks; their tragic heroes could only suffer and accept, thereby gaining the begrudged approval of the gods. Christian mysticism makes much more available to Hamlet, and Renaissance humanism makes Hamlet the transcendent artist: God created the world out of nothing; Hamlet sees the world is nothing; by contradicting the nothing that is the flesh his mother made him, he creates himself in the world of art. It is not unlike the immortality the Poet offers the Fair Youth of the *Sonnets*. As Fineman has shown, the *Sonnets* argue that poetry can lie, so writing poetry is not an imitation of the world as it is, but rather an imitation of the artistic process of writing poetry. In the *Sonnets*, the Poet uses his art to create the Fair Youth, but he constantly reminds the Fair Youth that it is the art of poetry that makes of him a monument for future generations to admire. In *Hamlet* Shakespeare collapses the two *personae* of the *Sonnets*—Poet and Fair Youth—into one, Hamlet, who praises himself and makes a monument of himself. In both *Hamlet* and the *Sonnets* there is a Dark Lady, a misogynistic fantasy of a woman who is only flesh, only of this world, and thus a threatening contradiction of all the Poet's pretenses to immortality: Eve in the Garden. In the *Sonnets* she is only mistress, but in *Hamlet* she is both mother and intended wife. Hamlet renounces his misogyny and his metaphysics in his farewells to Ophelia and Gertrude, but in his final instructions to Horatio, he bequeaths to him his artistic spirit.

5

CRITICAL APPROACHES

The first century of the history of *Hamlet* in criticism is based almost exclusively on performance. Comments are made on the actors' demeanor and the staging of the action; through these we can detect some reponse of an ethical nature. Then in the early eighteenth century, when edited versions of Shakespeare's plays began to appear, *Hamlet* became the subject of literary criticism; hence the comments of Pope, Johnson, and Coleridge. In this period, the focus of attention shifts from the shape and structure of the play to the character of the protagonist. This approach reaches a climax at the end of the nineteenth century, with A. C. Bradley's *Shakespearean Tragedy* (1905). In the first half of this century, a wide range of critical schools developed: attention was focused on the themes and imagery of the poetry, on the cultural background, on archetypal patterns of action and the psychology of the characters. Finally, in the past fifty years, various theories of literature and its relations with politics, philosophy, and economics have been applied to *Hamlet*, so that we have readings by feminist critics, psychoanalytic critics, New Historicists, deconstructionists, and others. I shall here chart the divergences and congruences of these various approaches.

Richard Burbage created the role originally in Shakespeare's company and continued to play it until his death in 1619. He is thus remembered in an anonymous eulogy:

> young Hamlet, old Hieronimo,
> King Lear, the grieved Moor, and more beside
> That lived in him have now forever died.
> Oft have I seen him leap into the grave,
> Suiting the person which he seemed to have
> Of a sad lover with so true an eye
> That there, I would have sworn, he meant to die. (Chambers, ii, 309)

When the theatres reopened in 1660 after the civil wars, the play was again in production, and the sequence of actors who performed the title role is unbroken. John Downes writes in 1708:

The tragedy of *Hamlet;* Hamlet being performed by Mr. Betterton. Sir William [Davenant] (having seen Mr. Taylor of the Black-Friars Company act it, who being instructed by the author Mr. Shakespeare) taught Mr. Betterton in every particle of it; which by his exact performance of it, gained him esteem and reputation, superlative to all other plays. . . . No succeeding tragedy got more reputation or money to the company than this. (quoted in Taylor 14)

Joseph Taylor, who joined the company three years after Shakespeare's death, was clearly brought in to replace Burbage. Betterton's last performance was in 1709. Thus, for over one hundred years, the role of Hamlet was "in the family" of Shakespeare's company.

In that same year, Nicholas Rowe's edition was published, Alexander Pope's in 1723–1725 and 1728. In 1765 Samuel Johnson published his edition of *The Plays of Shakespeare* with introduction and notes. Though he addresses the reading audience, he gives the impression of a stage performance to which he responds, in its full range of dramatic effects and richness of detail. His observations predict the concerns of future critics.

We must allow to the tragedy of *Hamlet* the praise of variety. The incidents are so numerous, that the argument of the play would make a long tale. The scenes are interchangeably diversified with merriment and solemnity. . . . New characters appear from time to time in continual succession, exhibiting various forms of life and particular modes of conversation. The pretended madness of Hamlet causes much mirth, the mournful distraction of Ophelia fills the heart with tenderness, and every personage produces the effect intended, from the apparition that in the first act chills the blood with horror, to the fop in the last, that exposes affectation to just contempt. . . . Of the feigned madness of Hamlet there appears no adequate cause, for he does nothing which he might not have done with the reputation of sanity. He plays the madman most, when he treats Ophelia with so much rudeness, which seems to be useless and wanton cruelty.

Hamlet is, through the whole play, rather an instrument than an agent. After he has, by the strategem of the play, convicted the King, he makes no attempt to punish him, and his death is at last effected by an incident which Hamlet has no part in producing. (Johnson 302–3)

His point here is that Hamlet is the instrument of the Ghost, not acting on his own. He thus raises the issue of Hamlet's delay. It is this that Coleridge, in 1811–1812, seizes upon and makes the focus of his attention: he asks what is wrong with the character of Hamlet. In this he follows the German critics

Goethe and Schlegel, who had called attention to Hamlet's intellectual nature, contrasting him with the more conventionally heroic man of action. We should recognize here a preoccupation of the romantic period. In their heroes, they reconstruct the melancholy types of the Elizabethan period. Goethe's Young Werther, who languishes in love for a woman already happily married and despises the members of the nobility on whom he depends for a living, finally commits suicide. Byron's heroes show a similar disaffection. The German philosopher Hegel defines the type precisely so as to illustrate both the similarity with Hamlet and also the refusal to recognize one's place in the world, an issue that has reemerged recently in Marxist criticism of Hamlet. Of the romantic spirit, or "Beautiful Soul," he says:

It lives in dread of staining the radiance of its inner being by action and existence. And to preserve the purity of its heart, it flees from contact with actuality, and steadfastly perseveres in a state of self-willed impotence to renounce a self which is pared away to the last point of abstraction, and to give itself substantial existence, or, in other words, to transform its thought into being, and commit itself to absolute distinction. The hollow object, which it produces, now fills it, therefore, with the feeling of emptiness. Its activity consists in yearning, which merely loses itself in becoming an unsubstantiated shadowy object, and rising above this loss and falling back on itself, finds itself merely as lost. In this transparent purity of its moments, it becomes a sorrow-laden "beautiful soul," as it is called; its light dims and dies within it, and it vanishes as a shapeless vapor dissolving into thin air. (*Phenomenology* VI.C.c)

Within the romantic movement, then, there was both the development of the individual to the point of his complete denial of the world from which he sprang, and the recognition that this form of alienation and superiority was self-indulgent and absurd. Perhaps it is this ironic recognition that separates the romantic from the Elizabethan melancholic, but we should remember that Shakespeare shows no patience with Jacques in *As You Like It* and, through the soliloquies and metatheatrical distancing, allows Hamlet an awareness of his own excess. This, then, goes beyond mere *Zeitgeist* to the serious issues of intellectual history. What is there in Hamlet that so aroused a whole generation of late-eighteenth- and early-nineteenth-century critics to identify his problem as the intellectual's remove from society and, further, to identify him with themselves?

This is the progress of Coleridge's reasoning:

The first question we should ask ourselves is—What did Shakespeare mean when he drew the character of Hamlet? . . . But the Ghost of the murdered father is introduced to assure the son that he was put to death by his own brother. What is the effect upon the son?—instant action and pursuit of revenge? No: endless reasoning and hesitating—constant urging and solicitation of the mind to act, and as constant an escape from action. . . . The whole energy of his resolution evaporates in these reproaches. This, too, . . . merely from the aversion to action, which prevails among such as have a world in themselves. (421)

He goes on to call particular attention to the altar scene (III.iii), where Hamlet has the opportunity to kill Claudius but decides to wait until he catches him in a moment more appropriate to eternal damnation. In the eyes of romantic poets and philosophers, Hamlet had become the representative of a particular malaise; for Johnson's generation, he had been a function of the action of his play. We have moved, then, in criticism, from the appreciation of character in the context of the drama—the Augustans generally thought of man as defined by his class, country, and circumstances—to the isolation of the hero who suffers because he thinks rather than acts, and because he thinks, he feels superior to those around him.

At the turn of the twentieth century, this preoccupation with the character of Hamlet had reached the point where speculation about him separate and apart from the action of the play became sentimental and naive. Bradley wonders about the young Hamlet, before the double trauma of his father's death and his mother's remarriage:

Still Hamlet had speculative genius without being a philosopher, just as he had imaginative genius without being a poet. Doubtless in happier days he was a close and constant observer of men and manners, noting his results in those tables which he afterwards snatched from his breast to make in wild irony his last note of all, that one may smile and smile and be a villain. Again and again we mark that passion for generalization which so occupied him. . . . There was a necessity in his soul driving him to penetrate below the surface and to question what others took for granted. That fixed habitual look which the world wears for most men did not exist for him. (17)

This sounds more like fanciful biography than literary criticism.

PSYCHOANALYTIC CRITICISM I

At the same time an entirely different, but perhaps related, method of criticism had its beginning in a footnote. In his *Interpretation of Dreams* Freud observed that the two greatest tragedies in the Western tradition had a common denominator, the Oedipus complex:

Another of the great creations of tragic poetry, Shakespeare's *Hamlet*, has its roots in the same soil as *Oedipus Rex*. But the changed treatment of the same material reveals the whole difference in the mental life of these two widely separated epochs of civilization: the secular advance of repression in the emotional life of mankind. In the

Oedipus the child's wishful phantasy that underlies it is brought into the open and re-alized as it would be in a dream. In *Hamlet* it remains repressed; and—just as in the case of a neurosis—we only learn of its existence from its inhibiting consequences. . . . Hamlet is able to do anything—except take vengeance on the man who did away with his father and took his father's place with his mother, the man who shows him the repressed wishes of his own childhood realized. (V.D.b.)

Hamlet hesitates to kill Claudius because Hamlet identifies with Claudius: Claudius has fulfilled Hamlet's own infantile fantasy of taking his father's place in his mother's bed. The theory was developed and situated in the tradition of *Hamlet* criticism by Freud's disciple and biographer Ernest Jones (*Hamlet and Oedipus*). Most discussions of it have focused on the problems it shares with Bradley's work—that it is fanciful in creating a childhood for Hamlet that the play does not provide. Also like Bradley, Freud assimilates Hamlet to a type. For Bradley Hamlet represents the disaffected romantic hero, whose sensitivity makes him incapable of action; for Freud Hamlet represents the power of the Oedipus complex—universally experienced by male children—to determine character. In fact, Freud's theory provides a useful gloss on several key scenes. It certainly explains Hamlet's confusion of sui-cide and the murder of Claudius in "To be, or not to be," and also the central-ity of the closet scene. In the first, we have a wonderful example of the power of the unconscious to shape the sequence of conscious thought, and of course it is in the soliloquies that we expect to find the character least inhibited in ex-pressing the deep structure of his thinking. (This is also true of the first solilo-quy: the imagery of "rank and gross" reveals the character's obsession with the mother's body and all its attendant guilt.) It has been objected of the Freudian interpretation of the closet scene that there is no original stage direc-tion for a bed in the room—indeed, that "closet" in Elizabethan English meant private library, or withdrawing space. Even though it might be anachronistic to present on stage that chamber as dominated by the bed, on which Hamlet can throw his mother as he rails at her, nevertheless, it cannot be denied that here Hamlet does intrude into his mother's private domain, and there abuse her in the most specifically sexual terms. We should also recall that his refer-ences to "incestuous sheets" are not confined to this one scene. It is fair to say that Hamlet shows a prurient interest in his mother's sexual activity. We might say of his expressed abhorrence of this what Gertrude herself says of the Player Queen's expression of devotion to her husband: he protests too much. This becomes an illustration of Freud's basic concept of *Verneinung*, "denial or negation." The unconscious mind makes material known to the conscious, but there it is censored. The stronger the id makes its contents known—"my mother's body fascinates me"—the sharper the ego's rejection: "my mother's body disgusts me." A similar argument can be made on the other side of the Oedipus complex: Hamlet's virulent hatred of Claudius, his reduction of him to subhuman monster, derives its energy from his own repressed desire to kill his father.

This much, then, is clear: only the most conservative (i.e., repressed) critics dismiss Freud's suggestion and the specific way in which Jones applies it to the question of Hamlet's delay. There is much more, however, in Freud's original conception and in other aspects of his remarkably elaborated model of the human mind, which can be appreciated in its application to *Hamlet*. First, it is historically specific: he distinguishes the cultures from which the two tragic masterpieces sprang. Since Oedipus actually does kill his father and marry his mother—though unknowingly—Freud reckons this as an indication that the Greek culture behind Sophocles could tolerate such a manifestation of incestuous desire and aggression. Since Freud's interest at the time was specifically dreams, and their revelation of the contents of the unconscious—to which he compared art, as revealing the latent fears and desires of the whole culture—he draws our attention to Jocasta's all but last words on the subject:

> What should a man fear whose affairs
> are ruled by chance, and he can foreknow nothing.
> It is best to live life lightly, as he can.
> You should not fear the marriage bed of your mother:
> Many men have dreamed before now—and heard from oracles
> —of sleeping with their mother. But he who thinks
> such things are nothing, lives his life most easily. (*Oedipus Tyrannos* 977–83)

Jocasta speaks these lines to the man whose essential virtue is intellectual curiosity—Freud was shocked when his students engraved a medal honoring his fiftieth birthday that depicted Oedipus solving the riddle of the Sphinx, a scene he himself had long taken to be emblematic of his career—and she contradicts the motto of Apollo, the god of poetry and philosophy, whose temple at Delphi was inscribed: "Know thyself." Freud compares Hamlet to a dream:

The prince in the play, who had to disguise himself as a madman, was behaving just as dreams do in reality; so we can say of dreams what Hamlet says of himself, concealing the true circumstances under a cloak of wit and unintelligibility: "I am mad north-by-north-west." (480–81)

This is not a facile comparison. Freud meant to suggest that Hamlet's madness, though feigned, reveals in distorted form his true emotions, as do dreams. He plans to kill Claudius, but cannot fulfill that plan; he abuses his mother for her excessive sexuality and cannot stop thinking about it.

In another of Freud's profoundly perceptive essays, he distinguishes between "Mourning and Melancholy." In the former, he argues, the patient goes through a normal process of gradually relinquishing the object of his desire when it has been lost to him. The energy invested in the lost object is then reinvested in the ego of the subject. In the latter, the process is complicated and incomplete. For the melancholic, the object has shown itself to be unworthy, but in withdrawing his erotic energy from the disparaged object, he introjects it into his own ego, so that "a shadow falls across the ego." This should remind us of Hegel's description of "the beautiful soul: "Its activity consists in yearning, which merely loses itself in becoming an unsubstantiated shadowy object." Hamlet's object is his mother, whom he disparages, but he cannot let her go; hence, the shadow that falls across his ego. We see then a conjunction of the psychologically specific and the philosophically general. The choice of the impossible object—usually incestuous, as Werther's obsession with his friend's wife—can be metonymic: *taedium vitae* is figured in the sexual relation. Even Hamlet's mourning for his dead father is abnormal: Claudius and Gertrude tell him that loss of fathers is "common," and wonder why his grief is so "particular." In Freud's model we can see that guilt and envy complicate his emotions. Notoriously, the most pathological mourning is that of the child who harbored repressed desires for the parent's death. These children are often haunted by the ghost of that parent. We shall pursue these issues in discussing the contributions to Hamlet criticism of those working in the psychoanalytic tradition two or three generations after Freud's original observation.

In 1919, reviewing two recent scholarly books, the great Anglo-American poet and critic T. S. Eliot made the charge that *Hamlet* is an artistic failure, since "Hamlet (the man) is dominated by an emotion which is inexpressible, because it is in *excess* of the facts as they appear" (25). It seems likely that Eliot knew of Freud's citation of *Hamlet* when he wrote this. He therefore obliquely suggests the difference between conscious and unconscious thought in art. It is precisely Hamlet's difficulty in expressing the cause of his malaise that makes his play so fascinating as a work of art. (Jacqueline Rose, for example, has referred to Hamlet as the "*Mona Lisa* of Literature.") It could be argued that only the more accessible, less profoundly disturbing work of art offers what Eliot requires here, an "objective correlative," "a set of objects, a situation, a chain of events which shall be the formula of that *particular* emotion."

BIOGRAPHICAL CRITICISM

In 1922 James Joyce published his masterful novel *Ulysses*, which contains a chapter in which Stephen Daedalus expounds a theory on *Hamlet* and its reference to Shakespeare's own experience. The chapter, entitled "Scylla and

Charybdis," is modeled after the episode in Book XII of Homer's *Odyssey*, where the hero must steer his ship between the two threatening forces of the monster Scylla, who will snatch his men from the decks and eat them, and the whirlpool Charybdis, which will swallow his ship whole.

Stephen is in a library and addresses the men of Dublin's learned establishment. His comments are a mixture of the perceptive and the absurd, a parody of dilettantish criticism. Among its remarkable features is the claim, "Hamlet is his own father." The explanation to this riddle lies in Stephen's contention that Shakespeare, as a young man, suffered the adultery of his wife, Anne Hathaway, as did Hamlet's father suffer the adultery of his wife Gertrude. He emphasizes that Shakespeare was younger than his wife and that their first child was born too soon after their marriage, so he was probably forced into it. That child was Susanna. Two years later (1585) the twins, Hamnet and Judith, were born. Shakespeare departed for London soon after. Hamnet died in 1596. Joyce has Stephen quote with approval the opinion of the French poet Mallarmé that Hamlet is a narcissist: "He walks about reading the book of himself." Also he kills without conscience: something in his self-absorption makes him insensitive to the suffering of others. Joyce's stream-of-consciousness style allows Stephen to associate seemingly unrelated events, both literary and biographical: Stephen, Hamlet, Odysseus, Shakespeare, Joyce; Gertrude, Anne Hathaway, Scylla and Charybdis (almost all the creatures who inhibit Odysseus's homecoming are female, e.g., Circe, Calypso, Nausicaa, the Sirens). We should also recall that the journey of Joyce's hero, Leopold Bloom, will end with his adulterous wife, Molly, the fulfillment of Odysseus's worst fear about Penelope. What Joyce offers us, then, is the collocation of an overwhelming woman, both older and sexually promiscuous, with a young man who is withdrawn, self-absorbed, and "anaesthetic." We shall soon see that these are the characteristics—in the mother and in the male child—that later psychoanalytic critics try to relate to each other. In the meantime we should acknowledge that Joyce's insight into the patterns of Shakespeare's drama, as related to biographical detail, is elsewhere shown profound. He explains Shakespeare's late romances as the attempt by the father to find in his daughter both the love he formerly had for his wife and a higher love that transcends others and restores to him "his own image."

ARCHETYPAL CRITICISM

In 1930 G. Wilson Knight published his study of Shakespearean tragedy, *The Wheel of Fire*. In it he took the extreme position, which he later abandoned, that Hamlet, as "ambassador of death," throws the relatively benign state of Denmark into disorder. This, of course, is a continuation of the nineteenth-century absorption with the character of Hamlet and marks one final turn of the screw to his image as a romantic outsider: "inhuman . . . or super-human . . . a creature from another world." We see something of Nietzsche's *Ubermensch* here, or the "blond beast" marauding through culture and killing with no remorse, but rather with the satisfaction of self-fulfillment. This is like saying that everything would have been all right in Thebes if only Antigone had left her brother unburied. One outdated and simplistic notion of tragedy—that it leads through the sacrifice of the hero to moral order—is combined with another—that the hero is excessive—and the whole genre is turned upside down. Knight seems insensitive to the pervasive imagery of the play, which makes Claudius and Denmark, not Hamlet, "rotten."

FORMALIST CRITICISM

In 1935 Caroline Spurgeon published *Shakespeare's Imagery and What It Tells Us*. With elaborate graphs and statistics she argues that there are organizing patterns of imagery in Shakespeare's plays, and the predominant pattern in *Hamlet* is disease:

To Shakespeare's pictorial imagination, therefore, the problem in Hamlet is not predominantly that of will and reason, or of a mind too philosophic or a nature temperamentally unfitted to act quickly; he sees it pictorially not as the problem of an individual at all, but as something greater and even more mysterious, as a condition for which the individual himself is apparently not responsible, any more than the sick man is to blame for the infection which strikes and devours him, but which, nevertheless, in its course and development, impartially and relentlessly, annihilates him and others, innocent and guilty alike. That is the tragedy of Hamlet, as it is perhaps the chief tragic mystery of life. (318–19)

Here she restores to *Hamlet* criticism the basic notion of Senecan tragedy, which had been displaced from attention by concentration on the hero: tragedy shows even the hero, who, though superior to those around him, is nevertheless flawed like them and succumbs to the same fate as all others. Her work also marks a landmark in its close attention to the text. In the 1930s and 1940s in both England and America, a new approach was being taken to literature in reaction against the fanciful, biographical excesses we have seen in Bradley; it became known simply as the New Criticism. It owed some of its momentum to T. S. Eliot and other modernist poet-critics, such as Ezra Pound, who considered the image as the essential element of poetry—what set it off from other modes of expression. Spurgeon then expresses the conviction that in *Hamlet* imagery is not mere decoration, but the revelation of Shakespeare's deepest concerns. As we have seen in the consideration of rhetorical figures, it is naive to treat great poetry as substance expressed through randomly selected form; rather, in poetry, there is an organic relation between the two, so that Hamlet's sense that there is something "rank and gross in nature" cannot be expressed in any other way: he sees the world as a garden and the garden as his mother's body.

HISTORICAL CRITICISM

In 1935 John Dover Wilson published *What Happens in Hamlet*, which takes the reader through the play scene by scene and considers some of the perennial problems. As early as 1839 the German scholar Herman Ulrici had shown that Hamlet's hesitation to follow the Ghost's orders was consistent with Elizabethan belief: "It cannot be a pure and heavenly spirit that wanders on earth to stimulate his son to avenge his murder" (Edwards 34). Wilson returns to this argument and establishes that Catholics were less skeptical of such phenomena than Protestants. More recently E. Prosser, in *Hamlet and Revenge* (1967), takes the extreme position of asserting that the Ghost is a demon, and therefore a temptation for Hamlet to risk damnation if he follows its demand for vengeance. All of these critics warn us not to judge the action in *Hamlet* by the standards of belief in our own time. This is an example of glossing a text, or providing background to it, which can prevent serious misreadings.

Throughout the 1930s in Germany, Bertolt Brecht was producing plays of a new order, and at the same time building a body of theoretical and critical work that had reference back to Elizabethan and Jacobean drama. It is easiest to see his revolutionary concepts as anti-Aristotelian. In Aristotle's view of tragedy, the events succeed each other in an inevitable sequence. It is not so much the hero's character as the predisposition of the audience to impose order. For Aristotle, history is what actually happens, but poetry is what could or should happen; poetry has a regularizing, idealizing tendency. Brecht wanted to break down this distinction between history and art, to show that in both cases the choices men make are as much determined by social and economic forces as by character. He saw himself creating an "epic theatre," in which the structure of plays was episodic, and the action was characterized by alienation (*Verfremdungseffekt*). He used such devices as supertitles and generically named characters to call attention to the artificiality of the convention. The most radical effect of this kind of theatre is keeping the audience off-balance, unwilling to accept what they see on stage as inevitable or part of their own experience. It thus accomplishes in art what Marx demanded in history: that we see it as a dialectical process of change, and not a set and inescapable pattern.

If we read Brecht back upon *Hamlet*, we note the importance there of such "alienation effects" as the soliloquies and the play within the play. Much of the conventional debate, then, as to whether Hamlet believed the Ghost, or whether his delay was due to a defect of character or religious principle, adherence to the chivalric code or some new code of individual ethics—all this can then be seen as precisely the sorts of alternatives Shakespeare demanded his audience to consider. Hence we trace two distinct but related traditions in contemporary criticism—the one calling itself "metatheatrical" and concerned primarily with aesthetics, and the other "materialist" and straightforwardly political. From the former I mention only Lionel Abel, *Metatheater* (1963), and James Calderwood, *To Be Or Not to Be: Negation and Metadrama in Hamlet* (1983); and from the latter Jonathan Dollimore, *Radical Tragedy* (1984, revised 1989), though he avoids specific treatment of *Hamlet*.

FEMINIST CRITICISM

In 1957 Carolyn Heilbrun published an essay, "Hamlet's Mother," in which she argued that critics such as Bradley had completely misrepresented the character of Gertrude; these male critics had simply taken Hamlet's account of his mother as a statement of fact and ignored the evidence of the play itself. This is the first feminist criticism of *Hamlet* and contains all the most salient ingredients that this approach has subsequently expanded and developed. First, it warns us that criticism is biased by gender. The reading of a text is almost necessarily oblique, its perspective distorted by unconscious expectations. Male readers identify with Hamlet and do not recognize his misogyny as serious pathology that is both unique to his circumstances and endemic to the culture. Then, through careful explication of the text, Gertrude is shown to be "concise and pithy in speech" (11), suggesting honesty and perception, a correction to Hamlet's view that women are frail, because their reason gives way to passion. Finally, we are forced to consider in a new light the oldest prejudice against women: what is it that they do with their bodies, that, in men's eyes, is less than and antithetical to what men do with their minds? As Plato put it, men in their sexual relations with women produce babies, but in their sublimated relations with other men ("Platonic"), they produce philosophy.

Whence springs this bias against women for being of this world, honest and unpretentious observers of life as it is lived? When Gertrude says of the Player Queen, after her lengthy insistence that she will, as a widow, never remarry, "The lady doth protest too much, methinks," she speaks both for herself and for all honest persons: "Do not pretend that life can be lived by principle and precept; in its constantly changing circumstances, one can only adapt and yield."

There are various schools within the feminist movement in criticism. At least some critics readily ally themselves with the materialist cast of Marxist criticism:

Feminist criticism can never be merely formal because women recognize, out of the experience of their own repression, what a powerful weapon art, especially literature, is. Literature is a major component of the educational process, and that process, not biological determinism, shapes our destiny. In seeking to destroy patriarchal ideology in order to better the position of women in society, feminist criticism is a political act.

Feminist criticism is a materialist approach to literature which attempts to do away with the formalist illusion that literature is somehow divorced from the rest of reality. (Stoker, 326)

Perhaps Hamlet doth philosophize too much. Conventional critics since the late eighteenth century have said so, but the observation takes on new meaning in the context of feminist criticism. Throughout Shakespeare's career—in all four of the dramatic genres in which he created (history, comedy, tragedy, romance), as well as in his lyric and narrative poems—he always insisted on the superiority of experienced reality over theory or idealism. Thus, as early as *Romeo and Juliet*, he deconstructed the courtly love tradition: Juliet does not want to be worshipped from afar, as Romeo had worshipped Rosaline, but rather to be approached intimately and physically, to be treated as a woman of flesh and blood and desire rather than as a statue or an ideal, the Lady. It is unreasonable to assume that he would suddenly reverse his career and turn backward in *Hamlet* by validating Hamlet's dismissal of Gertrude as a whore. Rather we are to see him wrong, as we see Claudio wrong in *Much Ado*, Bertram wrong in *All's Well*, and Leontes wrong in *The Winter's Tale*.

Men who judge women by absolute standards—she is either a virgin or a whore—are wrong: they depend on theory rather than experience; they worship at the altar of what Bacon calls the "idols of the mind." It is strange, indeed, but true, that contemporary criticism—at the end of the twentieth century—has only now caught up with the epistemology ("theory of knowledge") at the end of the sixteenth century.

The materialist and political brand of feminist criticism—mostly British and American—is balanced and complemented by a more theoretical brand of feminism, based in the philosophy of language, which is primarily French (Wofford 208–10). The question is raised by critics such as Kristeva and Irigaray—immediately or indirectly influenced by the psychoanalytic critic and philosopher Jacques Lacan—whether women are adequately represented in the patriarchal languages of Western civilization. Language itself is seen as driven by desire: words represent absent objects; we speak only what we do not possess. But language is a system that alienates us from ourselves: it cannot express our own peculiar desires but only generic desires. We therefore demand the fulfillment of our desires in language, but this very expression cancels and/or sublimates our objects into abstract qualities. This is particularly true of the maternal object: the male child first speaks his desire for the mother, but then under the pressure of oedipal anxiety, she becomes the symbol of all his deprivations. As Lacan reminds us, we know ourselves only through negation: the male child's fantasized punishment for wishing to take the father's place in the mother's bed is castration. As in the metaphysical systems of Plato and Hegel, actual experience here and now is canceled and raised to higher levels, which are more and more idealized. The mother becomes the lady of the courtly love tradition, or that ultimate paradox, the Virgin Mother Mary.

The only other woman in *Hamlet* is Ophelia, and she too has suffered misrepresentation in the essentially male critical tradition. Showalter has recently shown that in the nineteenth century, Ophelia became the prototype of the hysteric: artists depicted her in romantic abandon, and actual hysterics then imitated her postures. More and more, in both criticism and performance, Ophelia is being shown to suffer under male dominance. First her father and brother force her to renounce her claim on Hamlet's affections, and then Hamlet abuses her for plotting with his enemies against him. The final break with reality comes with Hamlet's murder of her father. It is tempting to see Ophelia's madness, characterized by sexual fantasy, as a mirror of Hamlet's feigned madness. Following the Freudian perception that Hamlet identifies with Claudius because Claudius carried out Hamlet's own oedipal fantasy, we might see Ophelia's madness as induced by guilt: her father's death represents the fulfillment of her own fantasy to escape her father's rule to be united with her lover. Like Desdemona, Ophelia is no longer seen as simply the passive object of male manipulation; rather it is precisely the strength of her spirit that causes her to react so violently to her circumstances.

PSYCHOANALYTIC CRITICISM II

Psychoanalytic criticism of *Hamlet* began with Freud's *Interpretation of Dreams* (1900) and continues today. It is both the most effective application of Freudian theory to a literary text and the most persuasive explanation of the play's (and the character's) problems.

Freud's original observation, that Hamlet cannot kill Claudius because he identifies with him, since Claudius has fulfilled Hamlet's own oedipal desire to take his father's place in his mother's bed, was set within the context of conventional criticism of the play by his disciple and biographer Ernest Jones. Among other observations, Jones called attention to the anti-oedipal character of Hamlet's fantasies. He identifies with his dead father and has to be warned twice by the Ghost not to take hostile action against his mother. Classical scholars had already cited Hamlet's affinities with Orestes, who was required by Apollo to avenge his father Agamemnon's murder on his mother Clytemnestra, becoming thus a matricide. (We have already noted that both Hamlet and Oedipus enter their mother's chambers with their swords drawn.)

At the heart of Freud's reading of *Hamlet* are two related propositions that are fundamental to all his psychology: the powerful influence of infantile sexuality on the patterns of unconscious thinking in the lives of adults. Naive resistance to Freudian interpretations of *Hamlet* usually derives from failure to appreciate this connection. We are not meant to see Hamlet as a three-year-old child; rather we are asked to consider how his strange behavior in maturity might reflect the normal experience of early childhood. By definition, neurotic symptoms develop in the adult when a trauma occurs that precipitates fears or desires suspended in the unconscious since childhood. For Hamlet this trauma is double: "his father's death and [his mother's] o'erhasty marriage." Freud's insistence on the universality of the Oedipus complex—all sons desire to take their father's place in their mother's bed—helps explain the universal and seemingly similar appeal of Shakespeare's *Hamlet* and Sophocles' *Oedipus Tyrannos*.

Conventional critics falter when they misread Freud, thinking that he sees only sexual significance in the plays. On the contrary, both plays combine plots of a transparently sexual nature with intellectual and religious themes expressed in imagery that relates "carnal knowledge" to rational thought and emotional disturbance. In Sophocles' play, "seeing" and "knowing" are parts of the same verb *oida*, which is then found at the root of Oedipus's name, which also means "swollen foot." Oedipus has seen his mother's body and known her carnally; his virtue is intellectual curiosity, and his wife-mother Iokaste tries to inhibit his search for the truth of his identity by telling him, "Many men have dreamed of sleeping with their mothers . . . best to forget such things and bear life lightly." As long as Oedipus has sight in his eyes, he remains blind to the nature of his crime; only when he blinds himself does he begin to have the "insight" that has been the virtue of the "blind seer," Tiresias, throughout the play. Tiresias himself had lost his sight when he offended the goddess Hera. She and Zeus disputed whether the man or the woman had greater pleasure in sexual intercourse. They appealed to Tiresias for an answer since he had started life as a man, been turned into a woman, and then returned to a man. (The two occasions when he changed sexes both involved his interruption of the coupling of two snakes, which is usually interpreted as childhood curiosity—and jealousy—over parental sexuality.) Since he had enjoyed sex as both man and woman, he was the expert witness Zeus and Hera required. His reply, that if there were ten parts of pleasure in sexual intercourse, nine belonged to the woman, offended the prudish Hera, so she blinded him. Zeus could not undo that punishment, but in compensation he gave Tiresias "second sight." In both cases, then—that of Oedipus and Tiresias—a sexual crime is punished by blindness. Among the functions of "dreamwork" traced by Freud is "displacement": dreams disguise their content by displacing action from one object onto another. This is "displacement upward," or sublimation: the talion punishment ("like for like," as in the biblical "eye for an eye") for incest is castration, but here that punishment is displaced upward onto the eyes. The eyes are the organs of seeing, and therefore of knowing, so the Oedipus myth and Sophocles' play examine the relation between incestuous sexual relations and extraordinary intellectual activity.

In Freud's analysis, the male child gives up his claim on the mother when he recognizes sexual difference: he sees that she "lacks" a penis and thereby fanatasizes that he himself might be deprived of his penis by his father in retaliation for his claim upon her (castration anxiety). This "normal resolution of the Oedipus Complex" sets in between the ages of three and five and leads to the latency period, which lasts until puberty. With that sudden rush of new sexual energy, the adolescent male displaces his interest in his mother onto other women, sometimes remarkably like the mother. We might think here of the close relations between Gertrude and Ophelia. Not only does Gertrude twice announce—contradicting Polonius and Laertes who insist Hamlet is out of her sights—that she had hoped Hamlet and Ophelia might marry, but she also describes Ophelia's death. They are, of course, the only two women in the play. Most important, Hamlet's misogyny is displaced from his mother onto Ophelia: having convinced himself that his mother is a whore, all women are whores, including the innocent young Ophelia, whom he abuses in the nunnery scene, where "nunnery" carries a secondary meaning of "whorehouse."

Other details of *Hamlet* that might be related to Freud's theory of the Oedipus complex include the congruence of the relations in the royal family with the relations in Polonius's family: whereas Hamlet sees his oedipal desires fulfilled by his uncle Claudius, the father he actually kills is Ophelia's father, Polonius. We have already noted the close relations between Gertrude and Ophelia; both Polonius and Laertes inhibit Hamlet's desire for Ophelia and Hamlet kills them both; while the most obvious importance of Polonius's and Laertes' proprietary interest in Ophelia is their repression of her desire, it nevertheless creates the dynamics of a "female Oedipus complex": the daughter acquiesces in her father's sexual prerogative over her. All this is worked out in the intricate theme of madness: Polonius keeps insisting that Hamlet's madness is due to unrequited love for his daughter, when we know that the madness is in fact feigned, but even were it true, it is his father's death and his mother's re-marriage that unhinges him; Ophelia goes mad in fact, and this is due to her father's death, murdered by her would-be lover, Hamlet. The two cases conflated suggest the equation of madness with a father's death and unrequited love.

Shakespeare presents a similarly complex problem in *Lear*. There, two of Lear's daughters betray him and one is faithful; he goes mad. Of Gloucester's two sons, one betrays him, and one is faithful, pretending to be mad; Glouces-ter is blinded. Both of Lear's faithless daughters are sexually promiscuous, as is also Gloucester's faithless son. What is the power of the father to control and direct the desire of his child? Here we seem to approach the "Freudian myth" of *Totem and Taboo*: in the primal horde the father kept all the women for himself, so the sons rose up against him and killed him; this oedipal crime is commemorated in the paradoxical worship and then ritualized sacrifice of the animal by which a tribe identifies itself.

Other of Freud's treatises that also seem to have a bearing on *Hamlet* are "On Narcissism" and "Beyond the Pleasure Principle." We have seen that in "Mourning and Melancholy," Freud distinguishes between normal mourning and pathological obsession with the loss of a love object. In the former he sees the necessity for a "working through" of the grief: the mourner relives shared moments with the dead person and gradually separates himself from the other, narcissistically preserving himself from complete identification with death. In the latter, this is not possible because the relationship was not a "happy love" to begin with. Here the lover was not accepted by the beloved, so to protect himself, he disparaged the object of his desire, but so completely did he con-tinue to identify with the beloved that that disparagement reflected itself upon him, so that "a shadow falls across his ego."

It is not coincidental that Freud chose the same term for this malaise as Shakespeare did for Hamlet's condition. Melancholy is established in the tra-dition of philosophical and psychological writing before Shakespeare and continues throughout the romantic period and into the late nineteenth century to be particularly associated with unrequited love. I have already mentioned Goethe's young heroes Werther and Wilhelm. All of this can be traced back to the courtly love tradition founded by the troubadours of the twelfth century: the young poet chose as his object of desire the woman who was impossible for him to win—his master's mistress. So completely does the lover rely on the beloved to give him a sense of his own authentic being that when she is unresponsive or unfaithful to him, his sense of himself and of order in the world dissolves. Shakespeare's most compelling portrait of such a love is Othello's. Early on he confides to Iago of Desdemona: "Perdition catch my soul but I do love her, / And when I love her not, Chaos is come again."

In this context we can immediately see why Polonius is confused by Hamlet's behavior. The literary as well as the philosophical-psychological tradition insisted that the melancholic was unhappy in love. In Act I, scene ii, before Hamlet assumes his "antic disposition," Claudius and Gertrude complain that Hamlet's mourning is excessive: "Why is it so particular with thee?" Freud in fact interpolates a position between normal mourning and melancholy, where the mourner feels guilty for the death of the beloved. This, then, would support the oedipal interpretation: Hamlet's grief for his dead father is excessive because that death fulfilled his desire, and therefore he feels guilty. But the death of his father is not the only loss he feels. More pressing on him, as we learn from his first soliloquy, is the unfaithfulness of his mother: the world has become "rank and gross" because of her, "an unweeded garden." He mourns the actual death of his father, but also the image of his mother as chaste and pure, his fantasy of her before this double disaster. His wish for death—"Would that this too too sullied flesh would melt"—derives more from his mother's disgrace than his father's death. Freud therefore precisely describes Hamlet's melancholy: he has disparaged the object of his desire and yet continues to introject that object, so "a shadow falls across his ego."

In his essay "On Narcissism: An Introduction," Freud presents the argument that the ego can invest itself libidinally. Indeed he claims that this kind of object choice in maturity derives from the most archaic level of object relations: "The child has originally two objects of desire, himself and the woman who tends him, and the second leans up against the first." Here Freud's frequent insistence on the extreme selfishness of the very young child—"His Majesty the Baby"—and its tendency to promote its own well-being to the extent of ignoring or even harming others takes precedence over any inclination to push oedipal orientation back into the preoedipal period. The mother is first loved only because of her nurturing role, and not recognized as desirable in and of herself. We shall later see indications that even oedipal attachments are not pure and simple, but rather a function of fantasized competition with the father. That is, the male child's love for the mother throughout the early period of development is part of a dynamic of self-definition and assertion. Freud projects this dynamic forward into maturity in interesting ways that might remind us of Hamlet. First, he describes the cold, anaesthetic quality of the narcissist, unaffected by the sufferings of others, completely focused on his own narrow needs, determined to find some proper setting for his own excellence. This recalls the description of the Greek youth Narcissus himself as presented by Ovid in his *Metamorphoses* (III.339–510). He is beloved by both men and women, but responds to none; one of his disparaged lovers curses him, the gods hear, and he falls in love with his own image in the pool. There he retires to admire his own beauty, and he gradually wastes away because he cannot achieve consummation of his desire; finally the gods take pity and change him into the flower narcissus, which leans over the bank of the pond, reflecting its beauty back upon itself.

This reasoning becomes fundamental to Freud's later analyses of the structure of the psyche and the outlets it finds for its energy. He associates narcissistic orientation of desire, or ego instincts, with the death drive and the investment of libidinal energy in others with life itself. We cannot help but see Hamlet in the posture of Narcissus—remembering always that if there are ten parts of borrowing from classical sources in Shakespeare, nine are from Ovid—contemplating himself in the mirror of his soliloquies, insensitive to the suffering and death he causes others. His coldness to Ophelia, in particular, might recall Narcissus's treatment of the nymph Echo, who could only repeat the last words spoken to her and never initiate speech of her own: "Soft you now, / The fair Ophelia. Nymph, in thy orisons / Be all my sins remember'd." She then becomes the antithesis to narcissistic object choice: she depends on others to give her some sense of herself.

The other direction in which Freud takes narcissism is toward homosexuality. Homosexual object choice in maturity is structurally related to infantile narcissism, a sort of recapitulation. The clearest Shakespearean text on this phenomenon is the *Sonnets*, where the Poet seeks in the Fair Youth the younger, more beautiful image of himself, his nostalgically reconstituted, narcissistically invested self. We might also see in the Dark Lady some premonition of the fear and loathing of the mature female expressed in Hamlet's vision of his post-lapsarian mother. Twice Hamlet seems to be taunted with the specter of homosexuality: Claudius calls his grief "unmanly" (I.ii.94), and Rosencrantz and Guildenstern pick up on his innocent reference to mankind with knowing nods: "Man delights not me—nor women neither, though by your smiling you seem to say so" (II.ii.301–3). More important is his devotion to his friend Horatio, who serves as the antitype to the hypocrisy represented by Rosencrantz and Guildenstern:

> Since my dear soul was mistress of her choice
> And could of men distinguish her election,
> Sh' hath seal'd thee for herself. (III.ii.63–65)

Clearly, to the extent that Hamlet is capable of loving another, his object is Horatio rather than Ophelia. Later, when we project Freud's theories forward into the theoretical developments of his followers, we shall consider Horatio as Hamlet's "self-object"—one whom he invests libidinally only because he considers him a part of himself, inseparable and unthreatening, representing to Hamlet the very virtues—compassion and constancy—he sees lacking in himself.

"Beyond the Pleasure Principle" is one of Freud's most difficult and influential texts. It begins innocently enough with a bit of "baby watching": Freud observes his eighteen-month-old grandson, who he insists is not precocious, playing a game. He has a spool on a string, and as he throws it out of his crib, he cries, "Fort!" ("Gone"), and as he reels it back in again, he cries, "Da!" ("Here"). According to Freud, the spool represents the child's mother; so unhappy is he in her absence that he tries to manipulate his reality, pretending that he can send her off and bring her back by his own will. That the child would repeat painful moments of deprivation might remind us of the normal mourning process. Freud goes further, correcting his own earlier view that most of human behavior can be explained as the pursuit of pleasure. Now he admits that there is something beyond this and decides it is atavistic or phylogenetic. Pleasure is excitation that demands satisfaction; the organism seeks homeostasis, the restoration of equilibrium. This, like the attempt to restore the primary stage of narcissism, is nostalgic. The organism knows homeostasis only before birth and at death: there is then a death drive that takes us back to our preconscious origins. As Freud puts it, "Every living thing follows its own unique path to death." He also related the death drive to the Second Law of Thermodynamics: "Every closed system suffers entropy," meaning that if no new energy is infused, the machine runs down. He thinks here, as always, of libidinal energy: the subject who is focused on himself is death directed; only the subject who invests an external object with his energy and receives reciprocal energy from that object can continue to live.

Can we relate this mechanical model to Hamlet? He wants to die because the world has become for him "a sterile promontory." Perhaps we can see him regressing along a path that takes him back through previous stages of development. We would expect him, as his mother does, to move forward and choose a wife. Instead he rejects the fair Ophelia, having associated her with his mother, whom he now considers unworthy. All he is left with is Horatio, who might be considered that narcissistically constituted primitive object, the self-object, which represents the child's first attempt to mirror himself in the world. Indeed at the end of the play, Hamlet insists, again narcissistically, that Horatio absent himself from bliss a while (i.e., continue to live), to report Hamlet's story aright to the world. Horatio then becomes almost literally Hamlet's ideal ego, that corrected image of himself he would project to the world. We have already seen that Horatio also represents Hamlet's ego ideal, that figure in the world whom he chooses to emulate. We shall come to see that Laertes and Fortinbras represent Hamlet's aggressively invested self-images, those figures in the world with whom Hamlet must compete in order to ensure himself of his continued authenticity.

Moving from Freud forward along the divergent lines in the development of psychoanalytic theory, we might concentrate on two: the Anglo-American school of object-relations theory and the radical rereading of Freud by the French analyst Jacques Lacan, who is as much philosopher as psychologist. Melanie Klein, a German analyst who emigrated to England before Freud, first began to expand and elaborate Freud's theory of the relation between subject and object, emphasizing its dynamic interplay. Rather than continue to use such Freudian analogies as the amoeba's putting out its pseudoped to ingest a piece of foreign matter, Klein spoke of the subject-object relation as conceptual and interactive: the nursing child splits the maternal breast into good and bad objects and then introjects these objects so that he both projects his own emotions onto the mother (fantasizing the mother herself as ravenously hungry and therefore threatening to eat the child: the "Hansel and Gretel complex") and responds emotionally to his image of her, feeling guilt for his animosity and envy of her power.

Klein developed intricate techniques for studying the emotional life of the very young child, employing toys and patterns of play. She remained faithful to Freud's fundamental principle of investigating the images of objects that the subject forms and assimilates to rather than focus on what actually exists in the world—"real" objects.

Klein was followed in these paths of research in England by D. W. Winnicott and in America by Otto Kernberg. Winnicott insisted on the power of the mother to determine the child's image of himself: "the first mirror is the mother's eyes." Kernberg focused on the infantile origins of pathological narcissism, that borderline condition between neurosis and psychosis where the subject is not completely broken from reality (the psychosis of schizophrenia) but cannot quite distinguish the alterity of others (the neurotic relates with objects, but in obsessive and compulsive ways). The pathological narcissist can see others only as parts of himself or invests others as "self-objects." The classic case is the relation of Achilles to Patroklos in *The Iliad* (see my *Childlike Achilles*). Achilles sends Patroklos into battle wearing his own armor, so that when Hektor kills Patroklos, stripping the body and donning the armor himself, Achilles, in vengeance, must then face a mirror image of himself on the battlefield, essentially committing suicide by killing Hektor. (It is fated that Achilles himself must die soon after he kills Hektor.) We can then say that Patroklos and Hektor represent for Achilles erotically and aggressively invested self-objects, respectively.

We see something of the same dynamics in *Hamlet*. Doubling is the essential trope of the play, reaching up from the rhetorical level (hendiadys) through plot to character and theme. The play is full of sons who avenge their fathers: Laertes, Fortinbras, Pyrrhus (Achilles' son in the Player's speech). From the perspective of the analysts who emphasize the importance of very early childhood development, we might see such reverse images of Hamlet as a reactive formation against the power of the mother. Certainly we see Horatio that way. His relation to Hamlet is precisely the same as Patroklos's to Achilles: the honest, straightforward, perhaps slightly simple-minded, but wholly supportive friend who poses no threat of competition or antagonism. If, with Klein, we see Hamlet as having split the maternal imago into good and bad—she tells him in the closet scene that he has "cleft her heart in twain" and he tells her, "O, throw away the worser part of it"—the good is that image of the Lady of the courtly love tradition, pure and serene, maternal without being sexual, the Virgin Mary; the bad mother is the whore. The world is the mother's body, so it has become "rank and gross." Nature is simply "she who gives birth." It should not surprise us to find among Klein's works a study of Aeschylus's *Oresteia*. Clytemnestra is the whorish and murderous mother: she dreams she has suckled a snake, and it has drawn blood along with milk from her breast; this is Orestes come home to kill his mother for her having killed his father. Shakespeare has captured the same kind of mother in Lady Macbeth, who wants to unmilk her breasts, fill them full of gall, and would gladly snatch the child nursing from her breast and smash its brains out rather than break her word. Janet Adelman has studied this type in Shakespeare in her *Suffocating Mothers*.

Jacques Lacan disparages the object relations school of psychoanalysis, but many of his concepts can be shown to have been derived from its most important theorists. Everything is changed, however, in the prism of his extraordinarily complex system of thought. Intellectually, he is most influenced by the structural linguistics of Ferdinand de Saussure and the philosophies of Hegel and Heidegger. In 1959 Lacan devoted seven seminars to *Hamlet*, within a series devoted to the subject "Desire and Its Interpretation." Lacan reads the play as Hamlet's attempt to assume his own desire, to become the subject of desire rather than its object for another. Following Freud, Lacan speaks in terms of the phallus as the locus of desire, but he insists it signifies lack: "to be the phallus for the other, one must oneself be castrated."

Hamlet begins the action of the play caught in the desire of his mother. Here Lacan uses one of his pseudomathematical figures: $\$ \diamond <a>$. The subject is barred—deprived of authentic being—because he is subjected to the desire of a figure who has assumed for him the position of his own lost or compromised image of himself. His mother was the locus of his original conception of himself; he depended on her for reflecting to him, as in Freud's Fort-Da game, his sense of his own existence. In Winnicott's terms this would be "the transitional object," some perhaps originally tangible thing (like a blanket) that represents for the child an external, alienable self. This "thing" is he himself—we recall here all the uses of reflexive pronouns in the play— with which he attempts to fill the void he recognizes in the agony of weaning and the other processes of distancing that the very young child suffers. Melanie Klein had argued that the original object is the breast, but then the male child focuses on the penis, attempting to become that for the mother, whom he sees as castrated. Pre-oedipal and oedipal fantasies are merged or layered with each other so that the child would take the place of the absent father but sees himself only as his own fantasized image of the father, the castrated penis. Lacan claims that Hamlet's mourning is for this image of himself, which becomes merged in the graveyard scene with the dead Ophelia: he is not ashamed to make the equation Ophelia = phallus.

All this talk of phalluses is embarrassing and offputting for the non-Freudian, especially those with some sense of the patriarchal imperative lying behind Freud's original use of the term. It is important to avoid two attempts at revision when reading Lacan: one must not simply replace the phallus with the concept of power, and one must not ignore his insistence that the phallus signifies lack. The difference between the penis and the phallus is that the penis is a biological fact, but the phallus is a fantasy: it suggests power, but like everything else in the imaginary world, it is not what it seems but in fact the opposite. The penis becomes erect when the sexual desire of the male is aroused. This indicates lack: if the subject were complete in and of himself he would not feel the need of another. (One might think first of Adam here, and then of Jesus, as Hamlet so often does.) The phallus comes to stand in Lacan's analysis for the deprivation of authentic being that any thinking subject—notably Hamlet—begins to feel, but this is not just an amorphous, unconnected sense of inadequacy. Rather, it is specifically tied to and derived from early childhood deprivation. Lacan, like Shakespeare and the Greek tragedians, insists on materializing his metaphysics: their characters are caught in domestic situations (incest, parricide, etc.), and from these they extrapolate philosophy. If Lacan had known more Greek, he might have seen that Ophelia's name can be etymologized from *opheilo*, "to owe, to be obligated," which is frequently used in constructions denoting wish: "would that . . . !" In Homer it can be spelled *ophello*, which is another verb, meaning "to increase, magnify, swell." Probably unrelated, except through "false etymology," is *ophis*, "snake," that phallic creature crawling through the garden, who is responsible for all man's separation from plenty and completeness.

6

THE PLAY IN PERFORMANCE

Hamlet exists in three dimensions: text, performance, and cultural icon. In our examination of the different early editions of the play, we considered the probability that the Second Quarto represents Shakespeare's own original version of the play and that the First Folio represents the play as it was performed during his lifetime, perhaps with his own cuts and alterations. The First Quarto represents an "actor's memorial reconstruction," an effort by one or more actors to reconstruct the text from performance. We are extremely fortunate to have these different insights into actual performances of the play in the early seventeenth century.

The first production of *Hamlet* would have taken place in the Globe Theatre, on the south bank of the Thames, near Southwark Cathedral, not far east of London Bridge. The original theatre on this site was constructed in 1599, exactly when *Hamlet* was first presented, from beams salvaged from the Theatre, which had been dismantled after a disagreement with the owner of the property on which it stood north of the Thames. In 1613 this Globe burned to the ground, during a performance of Shakespeare's *Henry VIII*, when a cannon was discharged from the roof. The reconstruction is thought to have followed the lines of the original, rising on the same foundations. In 1989, portions of these foundations were uncovered; in 1996 a second reconstruction of the Globe was completed on a site about one hundred yards north of the original. The architects and theatre historians responsible for this modern building relied on the excavation of the original for dimensions, but on various other types of evidence for the detail. Some of this came from other theatres contemporary with the Globe, such as the Rose and the Fortune.

The experience of watching a performance at the New Globe Theatre is the closest approximation to productions in Shakespeare's own day. Details of decoration, costumes, props, and blocking cannot be duplicated with certainty, but the overall effect must be similar. The only serious question that remains is the size and shape of the stage. For the Prologue Season in 1996, the stage was a very large rectangle, filling up almost half of "the yard" of the theatre (see photo 1). The pillars supporting the portico over the stage then divided it into three distinct areas, which proved awkward in the production of *The Two Gentlemen of Verona*, that opened the season, and careful analysis will show that the same would prove true for *Hamlet*. What we expect from the reconstruction of the Globe is an added dimension to our understanding of the dynamics of the play on stage. All along we could imagine from the text how the action would take place, but if we are reasonably sure that the shape and size of the stage are correct, then we would expect ratification of those predictions.

Approaching the theatre from the east, along the banks of the Thames, one is struck by the simplicity of the design (see photo 2). It is composed of twenty bays, three stories high, each built of large wooden beams fitted together with wooden pegs. These components are all rectangular, but the effect of the whole composition is circular, "the wooden O." Over the skeletal frame of the twenty bays is attached a network of woven twigs to hold plaster, the daub-and-wattle technique still used on half-timbered cottages throughout Britain. A thatched roof covers the galleries but leaves the yard open (see photo 3).

On entering the theatre, one passes through a low-ceilinged entrance to the yard, with three stories of seating galleries rising above (see photo 4). This inner space is eighty feet in diameter. One is reminded of other open-air theatres, especially the Greek amphitheatres and the Roman Colosseum. We know from excavations that the yard was covered with nut shells and pebbles, thus almost literally an *arena*, or "sand lot." We might also recall that identically shaped buildings were used in Shakespeare's time for the sport of bear baiting, in which the bear was tethered to a stake in the center of the arena and attacked by dogs. The stage, from this perspective, is an intrusion on the open, circular yard. It juts out at the level of the first gallery, and from it rise the two pillars that support the elaborate roof structure, which covers the entire stage at the level of the third gallery. (In hypothetical reconstructions the roof structure only partially covers the stage.)

Behind the stage is the area, concealed from the audience by a curtain, called the Tiring Room, where the actors attired themselves for their appearance on stage. In fact the Globe had a more sophisticated arrangement. This area immediately behind the stage was used for interior scenes, which could be revealed to the audience by drawing a curtain. This was then called the Discovery Space. The actors had their dressing room behind this area and on the level above. The Discovery Space was conventionally used for such scenes as take place in council chambers and the more public, or reception, rooms of private houses; it became known as the Study. Above this was an open gallery that conventionally was used for balcony scenes or bedrooms, and hence be-

Photo 1. Courtesy of Shakespeare's Globe

Photo 2. Courtesy of Shakespeare's Globe

Photo 3. Courtesy of Shakespeare's Globe

Photo 4. Courtesy of Shakespeare's Globe

came known as the Chamber. On either side of the Chamber were twin doors used for entrances and exits. Above these were windows. A canopy depicting the heavens was attached up under the roof, so when Hamlet refers to "this most excellent canopy, the air, look you, this brave o'erhanging firmament" (II.ii.294–1995), he uses a metaphor, but the actor describes the Globe in fact. This underside of the roof was called the Heavens, and the space beneath the stage was called Hell. In the stage, approximately between the two pillars, was a trap door. The Ghost of Hamlet's father will use this trap door to reenter the underworld—not hell, in his case, but purgatory—but again, there is a punning significance between what the actors represent the characters as doing and what they actually do themselves. Shakespeare constantly calls attention to the Globe, which is the physical setting of his players, to remind us of his essential conceit that all the world is a stage, and vice versa.

One way of appreciating the structure is to consider probable prototypes. Just a half-mile from the site of the New Globe, on the Burough High Street of Southwark, is a public house, the George Inn. It is the only remaining example in London of the inn with courtyard and galleries, which is thought to have inspired the architecture of the sixteenth-century theatre. The players would drive their wagon, or "pageant," into the courtyard of the inn, and it would then become their stage, with the spectators seated in the galleries above, as well as standing about in the yard.

Let us now imagine *Hamlet* on the stage of the Globe. We cannot go through each scene in turn but can concentrate on the scenes that most revealingly illustrate how Shakespeare took advantage of the many resources his playhouse offered.

Act I, scene i. Bernardo and Francisco appear in the space above and behind the stage (the Chamber); this was used, especially in the history plays, for the battlements of a castle. It is here, then, that the sentinels appear. For the moment we are meant to be on the ramparts of the Castle of Elsinore:

Bernardo: Who's there?

Francisco: Nay, answer me. Stand and unfold yourself.

Bernardo: Long live the King!

Francisco: Bernardo?

Bernardo: He.

Francisco: You come most carefully upon your hour.

Bernardo: 'Tis now struck twelve, get thee to bed Francisco.

Francisco: For this relief much thanks. 'Tis bitter cold
And I am sick at heart. (1–8)

These two are then joined by Horatio and Marcellus; Francisco exits. Marcellus asks Bernardo if "this thing" has appeared tonight, and Bernardo responds that he has seen nothing. It is clear that Marcellus has brought Horatio to witness what the others have already seen. Before he can describe a previous night's appearance, the Ghost enters, also in the Chamber. (If one thinks it is getting crowded in that space, the configuration at the New Globe offers a solution. Now the Chamber is an open gallery that extends all the way from one window to the other, so there could be a distance of fifty feet between the Ghost and the other characters.) We know that Shakespeare himself took this part. When the Ghost refuses to respond to Horatio's request to stay and speak, he begins to tell the others of reports of ghosts on the eve of Caesar's death in Rome; this is interrupted by the Ghost's second appearance. After it departs once more without speaking, frightened by dawn's first light, the watchmen determine to tell Prince Hamlet.

Act I, scene ii. This court scene offers two possibilities of staging at the Globe. Watkins and Lemmon suggest that Polonius and Laertes, with other courtiers, are discovered in the Study, by the opening of the curtain. They are seated at one end of a long table, with Hamlet at the other. Claudius and Gertrude, with attendants, enter the stage through one of the doors. Claudius delivers a long speech explaining his sudden marriage to Gertrude—that it was made necessary by the threat of Norway to Denmark's borders. He dispatches ambassadors to Norway to protest, then turns his attention to Laertes, who would return to his studies in Paris. Polonius, the king's most trusted councillor, asks his approval, and Claudius agrees. He then turns his attention to Hamlet, who finally moves down stage to confront his uncle, now stepfather: "A little more than kin and less than kind" (65). It seems more natural that the whole sequence be treated as a throne room scene, as it almost inevitably is in modern productions.

Courtiers begin to gather on the stage, and then Claudius and Gertrude enter with pomp and circumstance and seat themselves on thrones upstage center. Hamlet is downstage right while the king attends to foreign and domestic matters. He then moves stage center to respond to the king's request that he not return to Wittenberg. The only advantage to using the Study as an opening for this scene is the curtain; action on the ramparts would be immediately followed by action suddenly revealed in the court. But this might be a modern notion. There are three distinct acting spaces in the Globe, and these can be used in any sequence. The mere fact of actors' exit from one space and entrance on another alerts the audience to change of scene and passing of time.

Hamlet is left on the stage alone at line 129, to begin his first soliloquy, "O that this too, too sullied flesh would melt." He speaks this downstage center, directly addressing the audience, following the Elizabethan convention that a character who speaks on an empty stage speaks the truth. As Watkins and Lemmon point out, this marks a sharp contrast with the hypocrisy of the court in the previous scene, perhaps the most consistent and important contrast in the play. He is joined by Horatio, Marcellus, and Bernardo, who tell him of the Ghost's appearance to them the night before. Presumably they enter from the door opposite Claudius and Gertrude's exit. When they have agreed to watch together on the ramparts that night, they exit whence they came.

Act I, scene iii. There follows the scene of Laertes' farewell to Polonius and his sister, Ophelia. Watkins and Lemmon argue that this is imagined as an outside scene, perhaps at the harbor, since Laertes says his "necessaries are embarked." It seems more natural that this should be an interior scene, with Laertes and Ophelia discovered in intimate conversation in the Study, where they are then joined by Polonius. Laertes exits, and Polonius adds his own warnings to those of his son, that Ophelia should beware the attentions Hamlet has shown her. Then they both exit.

Act I, scene iv. Back on the ramparts. It would be unfair to ask even an Elizabethan audience to imagine a scene they had already had presented to them on one stage of the theatre, transferred to another in fewer than four hundred lines. If in Act I, scene i the ramparts are represented in the Chamber, then so too they must be in scene iv, at least initially. (Cf. Edwards in *The New Cambridge Shakespeare*, who reproduces the drawings of Hodges to show all the action of Act I, scenes iv and v, taking place on the stage.) The scene opens with Hamlet, Horatio, and Marcellus mounted to the top of the castle, awaiting another appearance of the Ghost, and meanwhile remarking on the king's wassail, as promised in scene ii: "But to my mind, though I am native here / And to the manner born, it is a custom / More honored in the breach than in the observance" (14–16). We might even hear the cannon being fired from the "hut" above the Heavens, but this would run the risk of repeating the fire of 1613. When the Ghost appears, it beckons Hamlet to follow (78), and though his friends try to prevent him, he does. Hamlet and the Ghost move quickly down interior stairs to emerge on the stage below. There is dialogue between Horatio and Marcellus to cover this action (87–91).

Hamlet is now alone on stage with the Ghost and hears his tale of murder and the harrowing of hell. It is precisely to hell that the Ghost returns with his line, "Adieu, adieu, adieu. Remember me" (91); he descends through the trap door in the middle of the stage. Horatio and Marcellus intrude at 113. Here the pillars rising from the stage could be used to advantage: Hamlet begins to take on his "antic disposition," and this could involve a sort of catch-as-catch-can between them. The Ghost thrice intervenes with the injunction that the friends swear to protect Hamlet by not revealing his visit (155, 161, 181). These cries come from under the stage, where Hamlet accuses it of being an "old mole." As Watkins and Lemmon argue, this makes no sense on actual ramparts, but only on the stage of the Globe: a mole could not burrow in stone, but could easily make its home beneath the stage. Again Shakespeare calls attention to his own conventions, challenging his audience constantly to compare the dramatic illusion with the physical reality of the performance.

At no point in this sequence of action is there need of more than one acting space on the stage. If a distinction of time or place is to be made, it is accomplished by a dislocation of the action from stage to Study to Chamber, never from one side of the stage to the other. This focus of the action at the center of the theatre also makes for the best sight lines. The extremely wide stage used in the Prologue Season at the New Globe does not offer acting spaces called for in *Hamlet*. It is only through adaptation to the modern proscenium stage that different acting spaces on the same level or on aprons slightly lower have come into use. These should not be projected back onto the original configuration of the Globe. There the stage was defined by the pillars; any area outside the pillars sufficiently large for an acting space would destroy the focus, which seems to have been one of its original virtues.

Richard Burbage originated the role of Hamlet and continued to play it on the stage of the Globe after Shakespeare's death in 1616, until his own death in 1619. He was succeeded by Joseph Taylor. William Davenant was the manager of the theatre when, along with all others, it was closed, at the start of the civil wars on September 2, 1642. It was demolished April 15, 1644. After the Restoration of the monarchy in 1660, when licenses to open theatres were again issued, Davenant began producing plays in an indoor theatre in Drury Lane, the Phoenix. Thomas Betterton began acting the part of Hamlet in 1663 and continued until 1709. During this period the staging of the play changed drastically. Davenant introduced movable scenery; women began to take the women's roles; more masquelike effects were sought with lighting and interludes. (In this account and what follows, I depend entirely on Gary Taylor's *Reinventing Shakespeare*.)

At the same time that Davenant altered the physical conditions in which *Hamlet* was staged, he also altered the text. Taylor has suggested that with the foundation of the Royal Society in 1664, a movement was consolidated toward a plainer, more uniform standard of English. Davenant changed Hamlet's line on finding Claudius at prayer in Act III, scene iv from, "Now might I do it pat, now he is praying," to "Where is this murderer? he kneels and prays." Other changes include the following: perpend/consider, coated/met, bray out/proclaim, In hugger mugger/Obscurely, Affront/meet, buzzers/whispers. Hamlet says resolution "is sicklied o'er with the pale cast of thought," but Davenant says it "shews sick and pale with thought." We can see the weakening of both thought and expression—what often happens in the revision that sets in with the copying of manuscripts or the typesetting of printed editions.

The conditions of performance continued to change. At the theatre on Drury Lane, the forestage area was curtailed, and stage boxes were installed. The actor and manager Colley Cibber comments (1740):

When the Actors were in Possession of that forwarder Space to advance upon, the Voice was then more in the Centre of the House, so that the most distant Ear had scarce the least Doubt or Difficulty in hearing what fell from the weakest Utterance. (Taylor 57)

Taylor adds:

In the seventeenth century the actors had been, by the very design of their stages, thrust into the midst of their audiences, vulnerable and palpable; in the eighteenth century they retreated increasingly into the upstage scenery. The old theatres created intimacy; the new ones, perspective (both visual and emotional). (57)

He also notes how other forms of entertainment were added to the bill:

Pushed back from the audience behind the proscenium arch; no longer foregrounded but on the same plane as the scenery; competing increasingly with both spectacle and music for the audience's attention—an actor's performance could easily become just one more set piece, an isolated demonstration of elocution no more related to the rest of the play than was the juggling or rope dancing that surrounded it. (60)

The eighteenth century was the time of the great editors: Nicholas Rowe, Alexander Pope, Lewis Theobald, William Warburton, and Samuel Johnson followed each other with their revisions of each other's text of Shakespeare. The difference between these published versions and those acted on stage became wider and wider. In 1772 the actor-manager David Garrick dropped the entire fifth act of *Hamlet* and simply had Hamlet burst in on Laertes in the midst of Ophelia's second mad scene (IV.v). We have already noted that Hamlet became the model for disaffected romantic poets. Wordsworth, Keats, and Coleridge all identified with him. Text and performance became two separate traditions of interpretation.

In the mid-nineteenth century, such truncated versions of the play were performed for audiences who were less interested in the structure of the play than in its set pieces. The soliloquies began to be delivered like arias in an opera. The action comes to a halt, and the actor delivers his lines as though they had no reference to the character he plays in the rest of the play. Also, there was a developing interest in the historical accuracy of set designs. This was not an attempt to return to the Globe but, on the contrary, to return to Elsinore. Sets became larger and more elaborate so that the actors sometimes seemed to be lost in vast alien spaces. (We might refer here to Aristotle, who warns that spectacle should be the least important element of tragedy.) *Hamlet* was often performed in America during this period, by both native companies and touring British companies. On May 10, 1849, a riot broke out in Astor Place, New York City, when supporters of the American actor Edwin Forrest protested the appearance of the British actor Charles Macready; thirty-eight people were killed. During the 1857–1858 season in New York, there were ten different productions of *Hamlet*.

In 1874 Frederick Furnivall founded the New Shakespeare Society; his announced intention was to apply to the texts of Shakespeare the kind of analysis that characterizes the physical sciences. He was particularly concerned with putting the plays in chronological order, "for the purpose of studying the progress and meaning of Shakespeare's mind."

By the turn of the century, developments in several different areas, both specifically Shakespearean and more widely cultural, changed the standards of performance. Whereas during most of the nineteenth century the contemporary drama that was produced alongside Shakespeare tended to be sentimental, lending itself to exaggerated acting styles, and the players simply played everything alike, in the 1890s, first in Norway and Sweden and Russia, but then in England, a new, more realistic drama developed, and it began to occur to both scholars and directors that Shakespeare was completely different. There were certain stage conventions that he followed that do not make sense on the modern stage. In the soliloquies, for instance, the Elizabethan convention was that the speaker always told the truth, so it is absurd for modern interpreters to ask whether we can believe Hamlet when he says, upon finding Claudius at prayer in Act III, scene iii, that he does not kill him because he does not want to send his soul to heaven. At this time, the leading critics happened also to be the most distinguished poets and playwrights. George Bernard Shaw and T. S. Eliot both said patronizing things about Shakespeare, but they were part of a larger movement that was defining a new way of thinking about man's place in the world and how to present this thinking in drama. "Modernism" can be variously defined—probably most usefully as the refinement of form to reveal function—but in the theatre it meant a reaction against everything Victorian, especially sentimentality and "costume drama." A new style of stage design and direction developed that stripped away the accumulations of the previous centuries and replaced it with a starker, clearer vision. Thus by the 1920s, conventions of staging were closer to Shakespeare's own than they had been since the Restoration.

Shaw and Eliot both compared Shakespearean plays to musical scores, and the great theatrical innovators William Poel, Edwin Gordon Craig, and Harley Granville-Barker attempted at this time to produce them as a conductor would a piece of music—as an integrated composition where every actor played his part but did not call attention to himself. The director took control of the play away from the actors and forced them to subordinate their roles to his overall conception. The music of Shakespeare is the language, and its themes and variations the images that repeat and develop. In a radical departure from nineteenth-century theatrical convention, Poel produced in 1925 in London "Hamlet in Modern Dress." This marked the natural culmination of the tendency toward simplification of staging and concentration on the coherence of the text, but it also looked forward to the era of production when Shakespeare's plays would be set in any time and any place, to make the director's concept seem fresh and new. Taylor, in his detailed survey, presents the vivid contemporary contrast between the Royal Shakespeare Company, which, under pressure to produce six or eight plays each year, is always looking for something different, whereas the New Globe is obviously looking back, trying to understand how the plays originally worked on stage. This latter orientation does not mean that the New Globe will be a theatrical museum. Its first production of *The Two Gentlemen of Verona* was in modern dress and used some modern stage conventions. Rather, it means that its company is relieved of the burden of constant innovation. One would hope that future productions will be characterized by ensemble playing and a realization of the texts' potential for meaning as separable from any particular period.

STAGE

Among recent productions of *Hamlet* that have attracted popular and critical attention, one might mention that of the Almeida Theatre Company, directed by Jonathan Kent and starring Ralph Fiennes. It opened in London and then moved to New York in May 1995. As in other recent London productions (e.g., *Medea*, also designed by Peter Davison, and *An Inspector Calls*), the set first tells the audience the tone of the piece and continues to be a major aspect of the action, rather than just a backdrop, throughout. The rampart scene (I.i) gives us an apocalyptic appearance of the Ghost, with overwhelming thunder and lightning. The court scene (I.ii) shows an interior strangely raked to suggest towering portals and windows. This set is not built to human scale; the actors are incapable of filling it. Gradually we realize that this fits the director's conception: the world is running out of control, so the question is not, "What is wrong with Hamlet?" but rather, "What is wrong with Hamlet's world?"

As played by Ralph Fiennes, the prince careers about like a ball on a billiard table, well intentioned but all too human to control the game. He establishes wonderful rapport with the audience, stepping forward to deliver the great soliloquies, and rattles off "To be, or not to be," as childish gibberish. Unfortunately there is not a film or tape of this performance available; though such a record could never capture the intensity of the actual event, it would make further study possible.

TELEVISION

There is a readily available tape of the BBC made-for-television production, directed in 1980 by Rodney Bennett and starring Derek Jacobi. Kliman distinguishes three different approaches to a televised production: (1) those set on location that behave like conventional movies, with long shots and close-ups, shifts of time and space, and so forth; (2) studio-shot television drama with naturalistic settings such as hospital corridors and living rooms, shot mostly in middle range; and (3) bare-set productions with no pretense that the action is taking place elsewhere: we are even allowed to see the camera dollying in and out of range. Kliman concludes that the choice of the third style for *Hamlet* is appropriate: "Closest of all television settings to the kind of stage Shakespeare wrote for, the bare set can be stretched through creative camera work; such stretching is necessary to compensate for all that the stage has that television lacks" (196).

Shakespeare uses the aside and reference to theatrical conventions and equipment to remind his audience that they are in the theatre. The BBC *Hamlet* does the same with its medium, the television sound stage. Especially appropriate is the focus on Derek Jacobi as the prince. Kliman calls his acting style "bravura." The camera can pick him out and allow him to turn a moment in the text into a larger characterizing sequence, which is important when the text has been heavily edited: "moving images compensate or substitute for missing lines" (62). Kliman also praises the BBC production for capitalizing on elements previously admired by B. Beckerman of *Hamlet* as it would have appeared on the Globe stage: "[There is] a rising and falling action in each scene rather than through the course of the drama as a whole."

FILM

All contemporary productions—live, television, or film—are much indebted to Lawrence Olivier's 1948 film, for which he was both director and leading actor. Watching this film is an education in all aspects of performance: sets, costumes, lighting, blocking, music, actors' interpretations of the lines. All are impressive in themselves but also brilliantly subordinated to the director's concept of the play's central themes. Olivier gives us an essentially Freudian reading of the play; Ernest Jones, Freud's disciple and biographer, was consultant on the project and wrote an expanded version of his classic study, *Hamlet and Oedipus*, on that occasion.

We first note the artificiality of the set. As the camera pans down from the ramparts to the throne room, it lingers in the royal bedchamber, as if to warn us that this is where the tragedy is centered. No castle ever looked like this; no stage set could ever be so complex; it is in fact a combination between an actual location and a stylized representation, with the crucial feature of allowing the camera to move unobstructed "through" its walls.

Olivier was in his forties when he made the film, but chose for Gertrude an actress ten years younger, Eileen Herlie. She wears costumes that display her ample bosom, on which Hamlet often rests his head; they kiss on the mouth. Ophelia is the very young Jean Simmons, looking completely innocent and uncomprehending of Hamlet's misogynistic attack upon her. Claudius is played by Basil Sydney as pompous but robust, a believable rival with Hamlet for Gertrude's affections. From this nexus radiate out all the perfect details of conception and performance. William Walton's music is small in scale but dignified and energetic, capturing completely the spirit of an Elizabethan court. I have noted Olivier's extensive cuts and rearrangement of scenes, following essentially the Q1 "acting version." So necessary seem some of his decisions on blocking—Hamlet is aware of Polonius and Claudius's presence in the nunnery scene; Gertrude detects in advance Claudius's plan to poison Hamlet so drains the cup herself—that all later directors must consider them seriously before making their own. The film is best seen in its 16-mm format rather than on video. The cinematography, like all else, is masterful.

Of the two most recent films, one is little more than a cartoon version, and the other is some monster gone out of control. In 1990 Franco Zeffirelli directed Mel Gibson in an adaptation so truncated that Claudius, played by Alan Bates, speaks no lines at all, but only grunts drunkenly. Great effect is gained from Glenn Close, however, playing Gertrude. One student observed of the expression on her face in the opening scene, "Her first husband did not satisfy her, but now she is happy." Four hundred years of textual analysis have not produced so succinct and accurate an appreciation of Gertrude. Also, Zeffirelli has conceived the play in oxymoronic terms—Hamlet as an action hero—but it is not so foolish as it sounds. Rather than showing Hamlet moping about, enervated by melancholy, Zeffirelli has Mel Gibson bouncing off the interior sets and racing through the countryside on horseback: he has excessive energy, but it is all misspent.

Kenneth Branagh's film (1996) seems to have been based on several bad premises: compound all of Q2 with all of F1, to produce a text that folds over itself in bewildering repetition and contradiction; appeal to a general audience with spectacle and big-named stars in small roles; outdo and undo Olivier at every turn. Much is simply offensive. The Star Wars quality of the Ghost scenes undercuts their horror rather than enforcing it; the on-camera hara-kiri of Osric, played by Robin Williams, is probably the most outré and gratuitous alteration the play has ever suffered; Branagh's delivery of "How all occasions do inform against me!" on an ice floe with camera swirling overhead and torrential music washing around—just before the only intermission, which takes place two and one-half hours into the running time—reminds one of nothing so much as Scarlett O'Hara clutching her radish and saying, "I'll never be hungry again" (also the cue for intermission).

Nevertheless, there are wonderful individual scenes and splendid performances. Rather than simply show that Hamlet knows Claudius and Polonius to be behind the arras in the nunnery scene, Branagh takes advantage of a bewildering maze of mirrors built into the paneling of Blenheim Palace—his single set—so that Hamlet speaks some of "To be, or not to be" into a two-way mirror, which shows him himself, but allows Claudius and Polonius also to see his every move. Branagh plays Hamlet as intelligent, honestly perplexed, and appalled by the perfidy of his world, and determined to set it right. Derek Jacobi as Claudius gives a fine, richly textured performance, interpreting the usurper as a complex, disturbed figure full of contradiction rather than the conventional Machiavellian villain. Julie Christie makes us think that Gertrude is sincerely aghast at what goes on around her but unable to alter or affect the event. Indeed the production as a whole seems to suggest Benjamin's reading of the play as historical melodrama (*Trauerspiel*) rather than tragedy of character. It is the overwhelming force of history that distorts and destroys these figures rather than the flaws in themselves.

WORKS CITED

CHAPTER 1

Clayton, T. *The Hamlet First Published*. Newark: University of Delaware Press, 1992.

Kastan, J. K. ed. *Critical Essays on Shakespeare's Hamlet*. New York: G. K. Hall, 1995.

Raskin, N. *Shakespeare and the Common Understanding*. New York: Macmillan, 1967.

Shakespeare, William. *The Arden Shakespeare: Hamlet*. Edited by H. Jenkins. London: Methuen, 1982.

———. *The Cambridge Shakespeare: Hamlet*. Edited by P. Edwards. Cambridge: Cambridge University Press, 1985.

———. *The Complete Works of Shakespeare*. Edited by D. Bevington. New York: Longman, 1997.

———. *The New Folger Library: Hamlet*. Edited by B. Mowat and P. Werstine. New York: Washington Square Press, 1992.

———. *The Norton Shakespeare*. Edited by S. Greenblatt. New York: W. W. Norton, 1997.

———. *The Oxford Shakespeare: Hamlet*. Edited by G. Hibbard. Oxford: Clarendon Press, 1987.

———. *The Pelican Shakespeare: Hamlet*. Edited by W. Farnham. London: Penguin, 1970.

———. *The Penguin Hamlet*. Edited by T.J.B. Spencer. Middlesex, Eng.: Penguin Books, 1980.

———. *The Riverside Shakespeare*. Edited by G. Blakemore Evans et al. Boston: Houghton Mifflin, 1997.

Wells, S., and G. Taylor. *William Shakespeare: A Textual Companion*. Oxford: Clarendon Press, 1987.

CHAPTER 2

Benjamin, W. *The Origin of German Tragic Drama*. London: New Left Books, 1977.

Bright, T. *A Treatise of Melancholie*. 1586. New York: Columbia University Press, 1940.

Bullough, G. *Narrative and Dramatic Sources of Shakespeare*. Vol. 7. New York: Columbia University Press, 1973.

Burckhardt, J. *The Civilization of the Renaissance in Italy*. 1879. New York: Modern Library, 1954.

Burton, R. *The Anatomy of Melancholy*. 1621. Edited by T. C. Faulkner et al. Oxford: Clarendon Press, 1989.

Castiglione, B. *The Courtier*. Translated by G. Bull. London: Penguin, 1976.

Chambers, E. K. *William Shakespeare*. Oxford: Clarendon Press, 1930.

Coddon, K. "Madness, Subjectivity and Treason in *Hamlet* and Elizabethan Culture." In S. Wofford, ed., *Case Studies in Contemporary Criticism: Hamlet*. New York: St. Martin's Press, 1944.

Descartes, R. *Discourse on Method*. Translated by D. A. Cress. Indianapolis: Indiana University Press, 1980.

Devlin, C. *Hamlet's Divinity*. London: Rupert Hart-Davis, 1963.

Eliot, T. S. "Hamlet and His Problems." In *Selected Essays, 1917–1932*. London and New York: Harcourt Brace, 1932.

Fineman, J. S*hakespeare's Perjured Eye: The Invention of Poetic Subjectivity in the Sonnets*. Berkeley: University of California Press, 1986.

Foucault, M. *Discipline and Punish: The Birth of the Prison*. Translated by A. Sheridan. 1975. Reprint, New York: Vintage Books, 1979.

———. *Madness and Civilization: A History of Insanity in the Age of Reason*. Translated by R. Howard. 1961. Reprint, New York: Vintage Books, 1988.

———. *The Order of Things: An Archaeology of the Human Sciences*. 1966. Reprint, New York: Vintage Books, 1994.

Fraenkel, E. *Early Greek Poetry and Philosophy*. Translated by M. Hadas and J. Willis. New York: Harcourt Brace Jovanovich, 1975.

de Gilbert, J. *The Jesuits: Their Spiritual Doctrine and Practices*. Chicago: Loyola University Press, 1964.

Harington, J. *Nugae Antiquae*. Vol. 2. 1779. Reprint, Hildesheim: Olms, 1968.

Harvey, G. *Gabriel Harvey's Marginalia*. Edited by G. C. Moore. Stratford-upon-Avon: Shakespeare Head Press, 1913.

Hegel, G.W.F. *Phenomenology of Mind*. Translated by J. Baillie. New York: Harper, 1967.

Heidegger, Martin. *Being and Time*. In *Basic Writings*. Edited by D. F. Krell, pp. 37–90. New York: Harper and Row, 1977.

———. "Letter on Humanism." In *Basic Writings*. Edited by D. F. Krell, pp. 189–242. New York: Harper and Row, 1977.

Henslowe, P. *Henslowe's Diary*. Edited by R. A. Foakes and R. T. Rickert. Cambridge: Cambridge University Press, 1961.

Hobbes, T. *Leviathan*. Edited by Richard Tuck. Cambridge: Cambridge University Press, 1991.

Kristeller, P. Introduction to *The Renaissance Philosophy of Man*. Edited by E. Cassirer, P. Kristeller, and J. H. Randall, Jr. Chicago: University of Chicago Press, 1948.

————. *Renaissance Thought and Its Sources*. New York: Columbia University Press, 1979.

Kyd, T. *The Spanish Tragedy*. Edited by T. W. Ross. Berkeley: University of California Press, 1968.

Lodge, T. *Wits Miserie*. In *The Complete Works of Thomas Lodge*. Glasgow: Hunterian Club, 1883.

Loyola, Saint Ignacio de. *Spiritual Exercises*. Translated by L. Delmage. Hawthorne, N.J.: J. F. Wagner, 1968.

MacCary, W. T. *Friends and Lovers: The Phenomenology of Desire in Shakespeare's Comedies*. New York: Columbia University Press, 1985.

MacDonald, M. *Mystical Bedlam: Madness, Anxiety and Healing in Seventeenth Century England*. Cambridge: Cambridge University Press, 1981.

Milward, P. *Shakespeare's Religious Background*. Bloomington: Indiana University Press, 1958.

de Montaigne, M. *The Complete Essays*. Translated by D. Frame. Stanford: Stanford University Press, 1958.

Montrose, L. A. "*A Midsummer Night's Dream* and the Shaping Fantasies of Elizabethan Culture." In M. Ferguson et al., eds., *Re-writing the Renaissance,* pp. 70–82. Chicago: University of Chicago Press, 1986.

Nashe, Thomas. *The Works of Thomas Nashe*. Edited by R. B. McKerrow, with supplementary notes by F. P. Wilson. Oxford: Oxford University Press, 1958.

Nussbaum, M. *The Fragility of Human Goodness*. Cambridge: Cambridge University Press, 1986.

Plato. *Collected Dialogues*. Edited by E. Hamilton and H. Cairns. New York: Pantheon Books, 1963.

Rahner, H. *Ignatius the Theologian*. New York: Herder and Herder, 1968.

Skultans, V. *English Madness: Ideas on Insanity,* 1580–1890. London: Routledge and Kegan Paul, 1979.

Werstine, P. "The Textual Mystery of *Hamlet*." In J. S. Kastan, ed., *Critical Essays on Hamlet*. New York: G. K. Hall, 1995.

Vyvyan, P. *Shakespeare and Platonic Beauty*. London: Chatto, 1961.

CHAPTER 3

Aristotle. *Poetics*. In *Aristotle's Theory of Poetry and Fine Art*. Edited and translated by S. H. Butcher. London: Macmillan, 1920.

Bloom, H. *William Shakespeare's Hamlet*. New York: Chelsea House, 1986.

Cantor, Paul A. *Shakespeare: Hamlet*. Cambridge: Cambridge University Press, 1989.

Charney, Maurice. *Style in Hamlet*. Princeton: Princeton University Press, 1969.

Dollimore, J. *Radical Tragedy*. Durham, N.C.: Duke University Press, 1993.

Foster, Donald. "A Funeral Elegy: W[illiam] S[hakespeare]'s 'Best Speaking Witnesses.'" *PLMA* 3, no. 5 (October 1996), 1080–1094.

Handley, E. *Menandre (Entretiens Hardt XVI)*. Geneva: Foundation Hardt, 1964.

Melchiori, G. "*Hamlet*: The Acting Version and the 'Wiser Sort.'" In T. Clayton, ed., *The Hamlet First Published*. Newark: University of Delaware Press.

Miola, R. S. *Shakespeare and Classical Comedy*. Oxford: Clarendon Press, 1994.

Wright, G. T. "Hendiadys and *Hamlet*." In *Critical Essays on Shakespeare's Hamlet*. Edited by D. Kastan. New York: G. K. Hall, 1995.

CHAPTER 4

Abel, L. *Metatheatre*. New York: Hill and Wang, 1963.

Calderwood, J. L. *"To Be Or Not to Be": Negation and Metadrama in Hamlet*. New York: Columbia University Press, 1983.

Fineman, J. *Shakespeare's Perjured Eye: The Invention of Poetic Subjectivity in the Sonnets*. Berkeley: University of California Press, 1986.

Foucault, M. *The Order of Things: An Archaeology of the Human Sciences*. New York: Vintage Books, 1994.

Hegel, G.W.F. *Phenomenology of Mind*. Translated by J. Baillie. New York: Harper, 1967.

CHAPTER 5

Abel, L. *Metatheatre*. New York: Hill and Wang, 1963.

Adelman, J. *Suffocating Mothers: Fantasies of Maternal Origin in Shakespeare's Plays, Hamlet to The Tempest*. New York: Routledge, 1992.

Bradley, A. C. *Shakespearean Tragedy*. Rev. ed. London: Macmillan, 1905.

Calderwood, J. L. *"To Be Or Not to Be": Negation and Metadrama in Hamlet*. New York: Columbia University Press, 1983.

Chambers, E. K. *William Shakespeare: A Study of Facts and Problems*. 2 vols. Oxford: Clarendon Press, 1930.

Coleridge, S. T. *Selected Poetry and Prose*. Edited by E. Schneider. New York: Rinehart and Winston, 1962.

Dollimore, J. *Radical Tragedy*, Rev. ed. Durham, N.C.: Duke University Press, 1993.

Edwards, P. Introduction to *Hamlet, Prince of Denmark*, by William Shakespeare. Cambridge: Cambridge University Press, 1985.

Eliot, T. S. "Hamlet." In *Selected Essays*. New York: Harcourt Brace, 1932.

Freud, S. *The Standard Edition of the Complete Psychological Works of Sigmund Freud*. 24 vols. Edited by J. Strachey. London: Hogarth Press, 1953–1974. ("Beyond the Pleasure Principle," 18.3–64; *Interpretation of Dreams* 4–5; "Mourning and Melancholy," 14.243–58; "On Narcissism: An Introduction," 14.69–102; *Totem and Taboo*, 13.1–161.)

Hegel, G. W. F. *The Phenomenology of Mind*. Translated by J. Baillie. New York: Harper, 1967.

Heilbrun, C. *Hamlet's Mother and Other Essays*. New York: Columbia University Press, 1990.

Johnson, S. *Johnson on Shakespeare*. Edited by Walter Raleigh. Oxford: Oxford University Press, 1908.

Jones, E. *Hamlet and Oedipus*. Rev. ed. Garden City, N.Y.: Doubleday, 1954.

Joyce, James. *Ulysses*. Edited by H. W. Galdar. New York: Random House, 1986.

Kernberg, O. *Borderline Conditions and Pathological Narcissism*. New York: Jacob Aronson, 1975.

Klein, M. *Envy and Gratitude*. London: Tavistock, 1971.

Knight, G. W. *The Wheel of Fire*. 1930. Reprint, New York: Meridian Books, 1957.

Lacan, J. "Desire and the Interpretation of Desire in *Hamlet*." *Yale French Studies* 55/56 (1977).

MacCary, W. T. *Childlike Achilles: Ontogeny and Phylogeny in the Iliad*. New York: Columbia University Press, 1982.

Prosser, E. *Hamlet and Revenge*. Stanford: Stanford University Press, 1967.

Rose, J. "*Hamlet*, the Mona Lisa of Literature." In H. Bloom, ed., *William Shakespeare's Hamlet*. New York: Chelsea House, 1986.

Showalter, E. "Ophelia." In *Case Studies in Contemporary Criticism:* Hamlet. Edited by S. Wofford. Boston: Bedford Books, 1994.

Sophocles. *Oedipus the King*. In *Sophocles I*. Edited and translated by D. Grene. Chicago: University of Chicago Press, 1991.

Spurgeon, C. *Shakespeare's Imagery and What It Tells Us*. Cambridge: Cambridge University Press, 1935.

Stoker, F. Katz. "The Other Criticism: Feminism vs. Formalism." In *Images of Women in Fiction*. Edited by S. Koppelman Conillan. Bowling Green, Ohio: Bowling Green University Popular Press, 1973.

Taylor, G. *Reinventing Shakespeare*. New York: Oxford University Press, 1989.

Wilson, J. D. *What Happens in Hamlet*. Cambridge: Cambridge University Press, 1935.

Winnicott, D. W. *Playing and Reality*. London: Tavistock, 1971.

Wofford, S. ed. *Case Studies in Contemporary Criticism: Hamlet*. Boston: Bedford Books, 1994.

CHAPTER 6

Edwards, P. *The New Cambridge Shakespeare: Hamlet*. Cambridge: Cambridge University Press, 1985.

Kliman, B. W. *Hamlet: Film, Television and Audio Performance*. Rutherford, N.J.: Fairleigh Dickinson University Press, 1988.

Taylor, G. *Reinventing Shakespeare*. New York: Oxford University Press, 1989.

Watkins, R., and J. Lemmon. *In Shakespeare's Playhouse: Hamlet*. Totowa, N.J.: Rowan and Littlefield, 1974.

BIBLIOGRAPHICAL ESSAY

In addition to the various editions of *Hamlet* and of Shakespeare's complete works (see Works Cited for Chapter 1) there are other basic books that will serve to introduce students to the play. The best general introduction to all things Shakespearean is R. McDonald, *The Bedford Companion to Shakespeare* (Boston: Bedford Books, 1996). Its format is particularly illuminating since it juxtaposes documents contemporary with Shakespeare, such as the license for his company and his will, against modern interpretations of his world and work. Among biographies, the most recent and authoritative is S. Wells, *Shakespeare: A Life in Drama* (New York: Norton, 1995).

Several collections of essays give some idea of the vast range of opinion on the play: *Twentieth Century Interpretations of Hamlet*, edited by D. Bevington (Englewood Cliffs, N.J.: Prentice Hall, 1968); *William Shakespeare's Hamlet*, edited by H. Bloom (New York: Chelsea House, 1986); *Critical Essays on Hamlet*, edited by D. Konstan (New York: G. K. Hall, 1995); *Case Studies in Contemporary Criticism: Hamlet*, edited by S. Wofford (Boston: Bedford Books, 1994).

Among recent studies, I most admire J. Adelman, *Suffocating Mothers: Fantasies of Maternal Origin in Shakespeare's Plays, Hamlet to The Tempest* (New York: Routledge, 1992).

INDEX

About the Author

W. THOMAS MacCARY is Professor of English at Hofstra University. He has previously taught Greek, Latin, English, and comparative literature at the Universities of Minnesota, Texas, Michigan, and California, and at Columbia University. His previous books include *Childlike Achilles: Phylogeny and Ontogeny in the "Iliad"* (1982), *Friends and Lovers: The Phenomenology of Desire in Shakespearean Comedy* (1985), and *Plautus: Casina* (1976).